Where Are They Now?

POMPEY

Andy Pringle

Media House Books

First published in 2010 by
Media House Books
PO Box 466, Eastleigh
Hampshire SO50 0AA

ISBN 978 0 9554937 2 0

Printed and bound in Great Britain by Hobbs the Printers Ltd.

Introduction

There must be something mysterious lurking in the depths of Fratton Park that captures the souls of unsuspecting visitors to the ground and converts them to die-hard Pompey fans. My first experience was a fairly dull match against Swindon Town in the late 1960's but after 90 minutes, despite losing 2-1, I was hooked.

On that day the team contained the likes of Milkins, McCann and Hiron. We shouted their names from the terraces and they became part of our lives, but what became of them when their playing days came to an end? This book aims to answer the question but, to tell the truth, it is an excuse to take a nostalgic trip down memory lane and to remember some of the characters who made the club what is today. It is not meant to be a definitive guide or a 'history' book, but simply a light read that will hopefully put a smile on your face regardless of your age.

A project like this would not have been possible without a great network of support. I am particularly grateful to Jake Payne, Pat Neil, Lee Edwards, Roger Holmes, Neil Fissler, Andi Saunders and my long suffering family who thought that this ghost had been laid to rest many years ago. In about 1996, I compiled a 'Where Are They Now?' that covered all league clubs and proved to be very popular even if it was labelled the 'bog-readers bible' and 'anoraks almanac'. I think my wife has just about forgiven me for that flight of fancy, so please enjoy this book – it may be another 14 years before the sequel!

Andy Pringle
andy@where-are-they-now.co.uk

PS: Play up Pompey!

ABBOTT, Shirley

100 apps, 3 goals (1913-1923)
Career: *Derby County, Portsmouth, Queens Park Rangers, Chesterfield (1911-1927).* Centre half who later became first team coach at Chesterfield. Died on 26th September 1947.

Photo: Ben Angel
Anything familiar about the Azerbaijan flag?

ADAMS, Tony

(Manager between October 2008 and February 2009.) After an illustrious playing career with Arsenal and England, Adams progressed into management with Wycombe Wanderers and had a 22 game spell in charge at Fratton Park following Harry Redknapp's first departure. In May 2010 he agreed to become the manager of Qabala FC in Azerbaijan, which is being relaunched and financed thanks to an injection of millions of dollars from one of the country's richest men. His assistant is another former player with Pompey connections, Gary Stevens.

AGNEW, Steve

7 apps (on loan) (1992)
Career: *Barnsley, Blackburn Rovers, Portsmouth, Leicester City, Sunderland, York City (1983-2001).* Became manager of Gateshead in 2001. Has since coached at Hartlepool, Leeds and Middlesbrough, where he became first team coach in July 2008.

AIYEGBENI, Yakubu

92 apps, 43 goals. (2002-2005)
Career: *Gil Vincente, Maccabi Haifa, Portsmouth, Middlesbrough, Everton (1998-date).* The 'Yak' joined Pompey in January 2001, initially on loan and his goals helped secure promotion to the Premiership. Moved to Middlesbrough for £7.5 million at the end of the 2004 /5 season and was then transferred to Everton in August 2007 for £11.25m. *Nigerian international and has scored more premiership goals than any other African player.*

AIZLEWOOD, Steve

204 apps, 15 goals. (1979-1983)
Career: *Newport County, Swindon Town, Portsmouth (1968-1983).* Strong full back signed from Swindon in 1979 for a fee of £45,000. Has since returned to his home town of Newport in Gwent where he now practices as a Chartered Surveyor.
Welsh under-21 international.

ALBURY, William

26 apps.
(1956-1958)
Career: *Portsmouth, Gillingham (1956-1959).* Former Pompey schoolboy whose first team appearances were restricted during a difficult period for the club. In 1959 he moved to Gillingham for £3,000 and later played over 400 matches for Yeovil Town. Managed Waterlooville and had two years as player-manager at Botley before retiring. Later worked for Havant Borough Council in their Parks Department but is still a regular at Fratton Park and an active member of the former players' association.

ALLEN, Jimmy

132 apps, 1 goal (1930-1934)
Career: *Portsmouth, Aston Villa (1932-1944).*
The British transfer record was smashed in 1933 by Jimmy's move from Portsmouth to Aston Villa, for a fee of £10,750. Ran a pub for many years in Swansea. Died at his Southsea home in February 1995

ALLEN, Martin

46 apps, 4 goals (1995-1997)
Career: *QPR, West Ham, Portsmouth, Southend United (1984-1998).* 'Mad Dog' arrived at Fratton Park from West Ham in 1995 for £500,000. Started his coaching career as assistant manager at his home town club, Reading. Has since managed Barnet, Brentford, MK Dons, Leicester City and Cheltenham. Became a scout for QPR when his tenure at Cheltenham came to an abrupt end following accusations of racial abuse. The charges were subsequently withdrawn. *England under-21 international.*

ALLEN, Rory

16 apps, 3 goals (1999-2002)
Career: *Tottenham H, Luton T, Portsmouth (1995-2002).* Became Pompey's first £1 million pound purchase when he joined from Spurs in 1999. He was plagued by injuries and was forced to retire at the age of 25, three years and only 15 appearances later. Left the club to go and watch the England cricket team play in Australia before starting a new career as a civil servant in the Foreign Office.

ALOISI, John

66 apps, 29 goals (1997-1998)
Career: *Portsmouth, Coventry City (1997 - 2001).* Arrived on the south coast in 1997 from Australia via Standard Liege and then Cremonese in Italy. Terry Fenwick paid the Italian outfit £300,000 to bring Aussie striker to Fratton Park and he started to repay the outlay instantly, by scoring within three minutes of his debut. He went on to bag of total haul of 29 goals in only 66 games . A £600,000 transfer then took him to Coventry City but he was dogged by injuries and failed to re-capture his initial form. He has since played in Spain (Osasuna), Italy (Alaves) and now back home in Australia for Sydney FC. *Australian international goalscorer, who is on the cover of the Australian version of Pro Evolution Soccer 6!*

ANDERSON, John

86 apps, 43 goals (1933-1946)
Career: *Portsmouth, Aldershot. (1933-1947).* Joined in 1933 and scored in the 1939 FA Cup victory. Ended his playing days at Chichester City before becoming landlord of a pub in Crystal Palace. He continued to attend Fratton Park but died in 1987 at the age of 71.

John Aloisi
Photo: Smoomonster

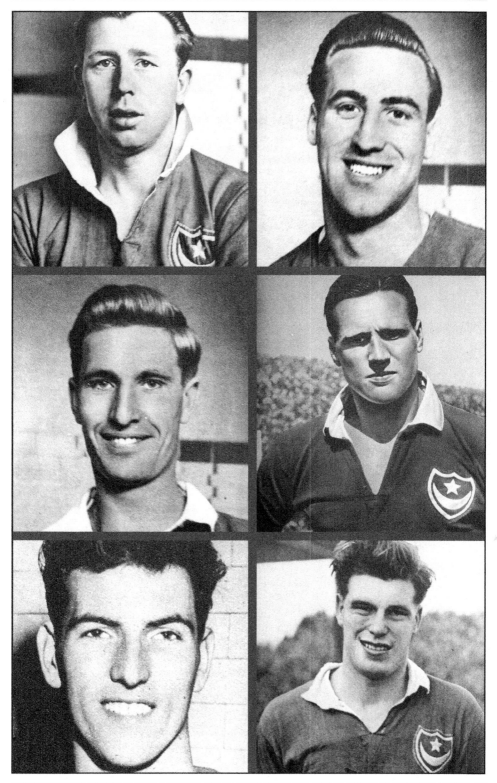

Where it all began - Felton House.

ANDERTON, Darren

77 apps, 13 goals (1990-1992)
Career: *Portsmouth, Tottenham Hotspur, Birmingham City, Wolverhampton Wanderers, Bournemouth. (1990-2008).*
'Sicknote" (a nickname apparently coined by Andy Gosney), joined Pompey as an apprentice in 1990 and quickly developed into a first team regular. He was one of the stars of the FA Cup run that was cruelly ended by penalties in the semi-final replay against Liverpool. His rise to prominence earned him a £1.75 m move to Tottenham Hotspur in 1992. He has since played for Birmingham City, Wolves and Bournemouth. Retired in 2008, but not before coming on as a late substitute in his last game and scoring the winner!
Won 30 England caps and was player of the season in 1992.

ANGELL, Brett

Pompey junior (1986-1987)
Career: *Played for fifteen league clubs including Everton and Sunderland (1986-2002).* Prolific striker who began his career at Pompey as a defender. He only started to shine when given the chance to join the forward line while at Cheltenham. After knocking in goals for numerous clubs, he finally returned to Fratton Park as a coach in 2005. This role only lasted five months and he has since coached in Ecuador and taught coaching courses for the Football Association before taking up a regional coaching job in New Zealand..

ARMSTRONG, James ('Joe')

78 apps, 31 goals (1913-1921)
Career: *Scotswood, Portsmouth, Sheffield Wednesday, Norwich City, Clapton Orient, Scotswood, Bournemouth, Portsmouth Trams (1913-1924).* Scored 15 goals for the Pompey side that won the Southern League Championship in 1919-20. Died in 1966. at the age of 74.

ARMSTRONG, John

86 apps (1963-1967)
Career: *Barrow, Nottingham Forest, Portsmouth, Southport (1955-1970).* Scottish goalie who played 86 matches before John Milkins emerged as competition and prompted his move to Southport. Managed New Brighton before leaving the game. Went into the frozen food business becoming a Business Sales Manager until he retired and moved back to Scotland.

ASHWORTH, Phil

5 apps, 4 goals (1979-1980)
Career: *Blackburn Rovers, Bournemouth, Workington, Southport, Rochdale, Portsmouth, Scunthorpe United (1974-1981).* A brief stay saw him score four goals in as many appearances but never established himself in the first team. Moved on to Scunthorpe and ended his playing days in Tasmania, having previously played in Sweden. Returned to live in Brigg, South Lincolnshire and to work as a delivery driver for a local stationery firm. His daughter married Hull City defender Andy Dawson.

ASPINALL, Warren

157 apps, 28 goals (1988-1993)
Career: *Played for ten league clubs including Everton and Aston Villa (1985-2000).* Joined Pompey in 1988 for £315,000 from Aston Villa. After several successful seasons, including the FA Cup run of 1992, he left for Bournemouth in 1993. A long term ankle injury forced him to retire in 2000, while on Brighton's books. Made the headlines when his drinking and gambling got out of hand, but happily, he has now recovered, found work as a warehouseman and has also helped out with some scouting.

ATYEO, John

2 apps (1950-1951)
Career: *Portsmouth, Bristol City (1950-1965).* Only played twice for Pompey but clocked up almost 600 appearances for Bristol City, and scored over 300 goals. A former England international, John qualified as a teacher and taught at a school in Warminster before suffering a fatal heart attack at his Wiltshire home in 1993, aged 61
A stand at Bristol City's Ashton Gate was named after him.

ATKINS, William (Bill)

11 apps 2 goals (1968-1969)
Career: *Swindon Town, Halifax Town, Stockport County, Portsmouth, Halifax Town, Rochdale, Darlington (1959-1974) .*
Tall goalscoring centre forward spent nine months at Fratton Park but only found the net twice during this time. Re-joined one of his former clubs, Halifax Town, for £12,000 in November 1969. At the end of his playing days, Bill bought a bakers & confectioners which he ran for thirty years. Now retired and living in West Yorkshire.

AUBEY, Lucien

3 apps (on loan) (2008)
Career: *Toulouse, Lens, Portsmouth, Rennes, Sivasspor (2001- date).* Joined on loan in January 2008 but did not do enough to earn a permanent contract. Returned to Lens and has since played for Rennes and Sivasspor in Turkey.
Played for France as an under 21 but Congo at full international level.

AWFORD, Andy

371 apps, 3 goals (1989-2000)
Career: *Portsmouth (1998-2000).* Before joining Pompey, Andy had broken the record for being the youngest player to appear in the FA Cup when he appeared as a substitute for his previous club Worcester City. He went onto become one of the club's favourite players and was constantly linked with moves to other teams. In the end, he remained a one club man until he was forced to retire due to injury in 2001. Even then, he stayed at Fratton Park - the role of chief scout was offered and accepted. He later became reserve team manager and then first team coach at Oxford United (under Jim Smith). Most recently managed Bognor Regis until January 2009. Awfs is now training to be a sports teacher and also shares his view of the game on BBC Radio Solent. *Andy played nine times for the England under 21 side and the 1997-1998 Player of the Year.*

AYRTON, Neil

2 apps (1979-1981)
Career: *Portsmouth (1979-1981).* Moved back to Maidstone United, his original club, after only two appearances. Having retired from non-league football, Ayrton established himself as a veteran runner with Blackheath & Bromley Harriers Athletic Club

Andy Awford

BAGLEY, William

139 apps, 13 goals (1933-1939)
Career: *Newport County, Portsmouth (1929-1939).* Despite having to have stitches above his eye during his Pompey debut, Bill went on to play over 100 games before the outbreak of World War Two. He was awarded an FA Cup winners medal in 1939 when he was first reserve despite playing in the first four rounds of the cup. During the war he worked as a storeman at Portsmouth Dockyard. Died in 1976 while on holiday in Scotland.

Photo: Paxie

BAIRD, Ian

22 apps, 1 goal (1987-1988)
Career: *Southampton, Cardiff City, Newcastle United, Leeds United, Portsmouth, Leeds United, Middlesbrough, Hearts, Bristol City, Plymouth Argyle, Brighton & H A (1982-1998).* Born in Rotherham but started his career at Southampton which took in nine league clubs and included a short stay at Pompey. He signed in 1987 for £285,000 but was sold back to Leeds United for less than half of the purchase price a year later. Moved into coaching, initially in Hong Kong, where he had a spell in charge of the national side. In 2003 he set up his own contract hire and leasing firm IBMH (Ian Baird Motor Holdings). Managed Havant & Waterlooville before taking over at Eastleigh in October 2007.

BAKER, Jim

Career: *Derby, Portsmouth, Hartlepool, Huddersfield Town, Leeds United (1910-1927).* Was on Pompey's books in 1912 but made his name at Leeds as a player and later as a director of the club. Died in 1966, aged 75.

BALL, Alan

(Manager between 1984-1989 and 1998 to 1999.) Career: *Blackpool, Everton, Arsenal, Southampton, Bristol Rovers (1962-1982).* The youngest member of England's World Cup winning side, 'Ballie' managed Pompey twice. Having joined in May 1984, he enjoyed three successful years and guided the club back to the old First Division following two seasons in fourth spot. Sadly relegation followed immediately and he was sacked in January 1989. He returned in 1998 to try and fight off the threat of relegation but his contract was terminated in December 1999. Earned 72 caps for his country and won a League Championship medal with Everton. Known for his white boots, he also spent five years with Arsenal, and had spells at Southampton and Bristol Rovers. His managerial career also took in Manchester City, Southampton, Blackpool, Stoke City and Exeter. He was awarded an MBE for services to football and was a popular after dinner speaker until his death in 2007. Firefighters were called to his Warsash home just after midnight on 26th April when his body was discovered. It is believed that he had suffered a heart attack after trying to put out a bonfire in his garden.

Photo: Dan Mullen

BALL, Kevin

124 apps, 4 goals (1982-1990)
Career: *Coventry City, Portsmouth, Sunderland, Fulham, Burnley. (1981-2002).* His career had started as a teenager with Coventry City but he didn't make the grade at Highfield Road and moved to Pompey in the summer of 1982 whilst still only 17. It was January 1984 when he made the breakthrough into the first team, appearing at right back in a 2-0 defeat at Shrewsbury. That was his only appearance in that season but did establish himself in the first team and had made well over a century of appearances when he made the move to Sunderland in 1990.

He appeared in their FA Cup Final side of 1992 and led them to two promotions into the Premier League, in 1996 and then again in 1999. His playing days came to an end in 2002 when he was released by Burnley. After a short spell out of the game he returned to join the coaching staff at Sunderland at a time when Howard Wilkinson and Steve Cotterill were in charge of the team. He was appointed as assistant academy coach and briefly took over as manager following the sacking of Mick McCarthy. Bally returned to the academy and he's now their youth team coach.

BAMBER, Dave

4 apps (1984)
Career: *Blackpool, Coventry City, Walsall, Portsmouth, Swindon Town, Watford, Stoke City, Hull City, Blackpool (1979-1994).* His last club was Blackpool (for a second spell) where he became a hero and entered into their Hall of Fame. You can even buy Dave Bamber tee-shirts from a site called cultzeros.co.uk. Dave remained in the area to become a property developer.
A Torquay United fanzine was named 'Bamber's Right Foot' following his penalty miss against the Gulls in the 1990-1 play off final at Wembley.

THEY'VE GOT SOME ROTTEN BAD SHOTS AT PORTSMOUTH

Another way to remember former players.

BARLOW, Bert
114 apps, 34 goals (1939-1946)
Career: *Portsmouth, Leicester City, Colchester United (1939-1954)*. Scored in the 1939 FA Cup Final victory on 1939 and a member of the 1949 Championship winning side. He later played for Leicester City and Colchester United before working in the family store and for a private car hire firm. Lived in retirement in Colchester until his death on 19th March 2004, aged 87.

BARNARD, Leigh
90 apps, 8 goals (1977-1982)
Career: *Portsmouth, Peterborough United, Swindon Town, Exeter City, Cardiff City (1977-1991)*. Former Pompey apprentice who played 79 first team games before leaving for Swindon Town on a free transfer in 1982. He made over 200 appearances for the Wiltshire club and helped them to promotion in 1985/86 and 1986/87. Finished up at Cardiff in 1991, where he played a further 69 games before hanging up his boots. He then studied to become a teacher and currently teaches Maths at Abbotsfield School in Hillingdon.

BARNARD, Mike
127 apps, 26 goals (1953-1958)
Career: *Portsmouth (1953-1958)*. Inside forward who played 116 games for Pompey between 1953 and 1958. Also played cricket for Hampshire and was a member of the team that won the County Championship for the first time in 1961. Became a familiar voice on BBC Radio Solent's local sports programmes.

The former Portsmouth Grammar School boy also taught Geography and Sport at a local prep school until his retirement.

BARNETT, Alan
26 apps (1955-1958)
Career: *Portsmouth, Grimsby Town, Exeter City (1955-1966)*. Goalkeeper and former Army Corporal who joined Pompey from Croydon Amateurs having been spotted by Jack Mansell, who was working as a football coach at a holiday camp at the time. His departure for Grimsby in 1958 meant that Pompey had to find a new secretary, the post had been occupied by Alan's wife during their stay on the south coast.

BAROS, Milan
16 apps (2008)
Career: *Liverpool, Aston Villa, Portsmouth (2002-2008)*. Czech international who made twelve appearances in a Pompey shirt before leaving the UK to play in Turkey for Galatasary. Milan was top scorer in the Turkcell Super League in the 2008/9 season. *Although he didn't score a league goal for the Blues, he did win the penalty that settled the FA Cup quarter final match against Manchester United in 2008. Milan also created Kanu's winning goal in the semi-final and came on as a sub in the final itself.*

Mike Barnard

BARRETT, Neil

26 apps, 2 goals (2001-2004)
Career: *Chelsea, Portsmouth, Dundee, Livingston, York City (2000-date).* Former Chelsea youth team player. Since leaving Fratton Park in 2004, Neil has played in Scotland for Dundee and Livingston, He signed for York City in June 2009 and played for them in the 2010 Conference national play-off final at Wembley.

BARTLETT, Gordon

2 apps, 1 goal (1974-1975)
Career: *Portsmouth, Brentford (1974-1976).* Former apprentice who made an immediate impression when he scored after coming on a substitute against Bolton in 1974. Moved to Brentford the following year having only made one more fleeting appearance. It was in non-league football that Bartlett later made his name when he became the youngest manager to lead a team out at Wembley. He was only 30 when his side, Southall, reached the final of the FA Vase. Has managed Wealdstone since 1995 and notched up over 1000 games as their boss.

BARTLETT, Kevin

3 apps (1980-1982)
Career: *Portsmouth, Cardiff City, West Bromwich Albion, Notts County, Port Vale, Cambridge United (1980-1993).* Things did not look good when he did not make the grade at Pompey. A terrific run of form whilst playing for Fareham re-ignited his League career. He eventually played over 400 matches and scored 162 goals. Retired through injury in 1993.

BARTON, Tony

144 apps, 37 goals (1961-1965)
Career: *Fulham, Nottingham Forest, Portsmouth (1954-1967).* A former England Youth winger, Tony gained experience as coach at Portsmouth, before becoming manager at Aston Villa. His coaching skills also took him to Southampton, Pompey and Northampton. Suffered a heart attack during his time at Northampton and died at his Southampton home on 20th August 1993.
Led Aston Villa to their European Cup final success in 1982.

BASON, Brian

9 apps (1981-1982)
Career: *Chelsea, Plymouth Argyle, Crystal Palace, Portsmouth, Reading (1972-1982).* Former Chelsea apprentice, but played most of his league soccer for Plymouth. Managed an hotel in Truro, Cornwall after hanging up his boots, then ran several pubs before moving to Daventry to work as a sales rep.
A former England Schoolboy international.

BAXTER, Mick

0 apps, 0 goals (1984)
Career: *Preston, Middlesbrough, Portsmouth (1974-1984).* Mick made his name in 200 plus games for Preston before going on to play a further 100 games for Middlesbrough. Alan Ball signed him on a free transfer in 1984 but ill health meant that he left to become Preston youth team coach before making a full appearance. He was diagnosed as having Hodgkins Disease and tragically died of a heart attack in 1989 aged only 32.
Mick was the brother of current Finland manager Stuart Baxter

BEALE, John

15 apps, 2 goals (1951-1952)
Career: *Portsmouth, Guildford City (1948-1953).* Died on 31st August 1995, aged 65.

Dave Beasant

Pompey's own James Beattie - this one never played for Southampton.

BEASANT, David

28 apps (2001-2002)
Career: *Wimbledon, Newcastle U, Chelsea, Grimsby Town (loan), Wolves (loan), Southampton, Notts F, Portsmouth, Tottenham Hotspur (loan), Brighton (1978-2004).* 'Lurch' came to prominence as part of Wimbledon's 'Crazy Gang' in the 1980's, and went on to make over 700 League appearances for a whole list of different clubs. Briefly joined Pompey after Aaron Flahavan's tragic death and played 28 games before moving on again. He played his last competitive game in the 2002-03 season for Brighton at the age of 43. Won two England caps but ironically one of his jobs since retiring as a player, was as goalkeeping coach to the Northern Ireland international side. More recently, he has been working as a coach at Glenn Hoddle's academy in Spain.

BEATTIE, Dick

133 apps (1959-1962)
Career: *Celtic, Portsmouth, Peterborough United (1959-1962).* Scottish Under 23 goalie who established himself as first choice keeper in the early 1960's. A disagreement with boss George Smith resulted in his transfer to Peterborough United for £5,000 in 1962. Ended his career back in Scotland and died at Old Kilpatrick in 1990.

BEAUMONT, Billy

70 apps, 2 goals (1907-1910)
Career: *Swindon Town, Portsmouth, Southampton (1906-1911).* Played over 100 games for Pompey before being transferred to Southampton for the princely sum of £75. Died in November 1911, having contracted pneumonia. He was only 28.

BELHADJ, Nadir

48 apps, 5 goals (2008-2010)
The marauding left sided defender/midfielder now plays for Al Sadd in Qatar.

BELLAMY, Jim

(Early 1900's.)
Career: *Reading, Woolwich Arsenal, Portsmouth, Dundee, Motherwell, Burnley, Fulham (1902-1915).* Londoner who played for a number of League clubs including Arsenal and Pompey in the early 1900's. His real claim to fame was that he went on to coach Barcelona between 1929 and 1931. Died in 1969.

Beresford still plays for Newcastle Vets

BERESFORD, John

132 apps, 10 goals (1989-1992)
Career: *Manchester City, Barnsley, Portsmouth, Newcastle United, Southampton, Birmingham City (loan) (1983-2000).* Remembered as a great left back, but also for missing a penalty in the 1992 semi final shoot-out against Liverpool. This is a shame because he was one of Pompey's most gifted players at the time. Manager John Gregory had snapped him up from Barnsley in March 1989 for £300,000 and it did not take long for John to establish himself as first choice left back. Exciting to watch, he was never afraid to push forward whether playing in defence or midfield. Consistently good performances not surprisingly attracted the attention of bigger clubs including Liverpool and Newcastle. John joined the latter for £700,000 in the summer of 1992, where he instantly won a First Division champion's medal. A £1.5 million move brought him back south to Southampton before retiring from the game in 1999/2000. He now works as an after dinner speaker and TV pundit for Tyne Tees TV and ESPN. He won two England 'B' caps but has also represented his country in beach soccer. *He has his own website, which has not been updated since 2006 but is still at: www.officialplayersites.com/players/beresford and will earn you a 10% discount if you want his mum to cut your hair!*

Life is so hard for ex-footballers.

BERGER, Patrick

60 apps, 8 goals (2003-2005)
Career: *Liverpool, Portsmouth, Aston Villa, Stoke City (loan) (1996-2007).* Czech Republic international winger. Returned home to play for Prague in 2008, but finally retired from the game due to injury in January 2010. *Scored in the 1996 Euro final against Germany.*

BERKOVIC, Eyal

28 apps, 3 goals (2004-2005)
Career: *Southampton (loan), West Ham, Celtic, Blackburn Rovers (Loan), Manchester City, Portsmouth (1989-2005).* Started and ended his career in Israel, his home country, but also spent almost ten years in the UK. He was brought to Fratton Park by Harry Redknapp, who had previously been his manager at West Ham. Retired in 2006 and became general manager of Maccabi Netanya. Although he only lasted two months in the job, fifteen players had been purchased in that time. (Maybe he learned a thing or two from his former boss?).

BERNSTEN, Tommy

2 apps (on loan) (1999)
Career: *Lillestrom, Portsmouth (1999).* A Norwegian defender who played twice for Pompey on loan from Lillestrom. Was appointed youth coach at Norwegian side, Lyn, in 2010.

BERRY, Steve

33 apps, 3 goals (1981-1983)
Career: *Gosport Borough, Portsmouth, Aldershot, Sunderland, Newport County, Swindon Town, Aldershot, Northampton Town, Maidstone United (1981-1991).* Having joined from Gosport, he made his League debut at the age of 18, but never established himself as a first team regular. Played in Germany, Hong Kong, and for a number of non-league sides. In 2009 was reported to be head of global recruitment for a market research agency and based in Paris.

BEST, David

56 apps (1974-1975))
Career: *Bournemouth, Oldham Athletic, Ipswich Town, Portsmouth, Bournemouth (1960-1975).* Wareham born Best joined his local club Bournemouth as a sixteen year old in 1960 and played for Oldham Athletic and Ipswich Town before joining Pompey in 1974. He signed in a £22,500 transfer from the Suffolk club and became first choice keeper for the 1974/5 season. His career then turned full circle, returning to his first club Bournemouth and then settling back home in Wareham, Dorset. Managed Dorchester Town and Wareham Rangers in the Dorset Combination League but now works as a transport manager for Westwind Air Bearings in Wareham.

BIAGINI, Leonardo

8 apps, 2 goals (2002)
Career: *Newell's Old Boys, Atletico Madrid, CP Merida, Mallorca, Portsmouth (loan), Rayo Vallecano, Sporting Gijon, Albacete, Arsenal Sarandi (1993-2008).* Argentinian striker who spent six months at Pompey in 1982, on loan from Mallorca. He played in Spain for four more seasons before returning home to Argentina.

BILEY, Alan

121 apps, 58 goals (1982-1985)
Career: Cambridge U, Derby Co, Everton,
Stoke C, Portsmouth, Brighton (1975-1987).
Much travelled, the blond haired striker finally
returned to the Cambridge area after a
career scoring goals for half a dozen league
clubs and several big money moves. Spells in
Ireland and Greece preceded his return to
manage Ely in the Jewson League. Business
commitments which included running his own
gym and health club "Bileys"in Biggleswade,
forced him to relinquish this role. Non league
management positions have since included
spells at Potton United, Barton Rovers, Diss
Town, Wootton Blue Cross, Kettering Corby
Town, Rothwell and Spalding (four times!)
Player of the season in 1983.

BLACK, Kenny

70 apps, 5 goals (1989-1991)
Career: Rangers, Motherwell, Portsmouth,
Airdrieonians, Raith Rovers (1981-2004). A
£350,000 move from Hearts brought this
Scottish midfielder south of the border. Later
became assistant at Kirkaldy, and then Airdrie
United in 2002. After a spell as coach at
Leicester, he returned to Airdrie in 2006, but
this time as manager. Relegation following in
2010 resulted in his sacking in June 2010.

BLACKBURN, Keith

38 apps, 8 goals (1960-1963)
Career: Bolton Wanderers, Portsmouth (1959-
1964). Keith is still heavily involved with the
former players association and has some
great stories to tell. Even though his league
career in this country was relatively short, he
managed to play with some of the game's
greats, both here and during his time in South
Africa. A Lancashire lad by birth, he started
out at Manchester United under Sir Matt
Busby and also turned out for Charlton and
Bolton Wanderers before accepting Reg
Flewin's offer to join Pompey. His stay at
Fratton Park meant that he played with Jimmy
Dickinson, Johnny Gordon and Ron Saunders
and was the proud winner of a Third Division
championship medal. He later joined South
African side, Durban City and was named
Sunday Express footballer of the year in 1964.
A friendly against Real Madrid also presented
the opportunity to play against the great
Ferenc Puskas. A bad knee injury meant that
he had to retire from the game and prompted
a return to Portsmouth area. He is now retired
and lives in Fareham, having enjoyed a
working career as a representative for a
snack company .

Keith Blackburn with fellow 'old boy' Alan McLoughlin

BLAKE, Mark

20 apps (1993-1994)
*Career: Aston Villa, Wolverhampton
Wanderers (loan), Portsmouth, Leicester City,
Walsall, Mansfield Town, Kidderminster
Harriers. (1989-2002).* Former Aston Villa
trainee, joined Pompey in August 1993 for
£400,000 as part of the deal that took Guy
Whittingham to Villa Park. He only stayed for
eight months, before moving back to the
Midlands and Leicester City. Retired from the
game in 2002 following a serious knee injury.
Won nine England under 21 caps.

BLAKE, Noel

168 apps, 13 goals (1984-1988)
*Career: Aston Villa, Shrewsbury Town (loan),
Birmingham City, Portsmouth, Leeds United,
Stoke City, Bradford City, Exeter City. (1979-
2001).* Blakey was the cornerstone of many a
Pompey defence in the 1980's. Born in
Kingston, Jamaica, his 6ft 2in frame provided
an intimidating challenge for opposing
strikers. After 168 appearances in a Pompey
shirt he moved on to Leeds United in 1988. It
was at his last club, Exeter City, where he
made his first management step when he was
appointed player-manager in 2000. He has
since made a name for himself as a
successful youth coach. Currently lives in
Newcastle-under-Lyme and works as one of
the Football Association's A's coaches and
works with the England youth teams as well
as helping educate new coaches.
Player of the season in 1986 and 1987.

BLANT, Colin

73 apps, 1 goal (1970-1972)
*Career: Burnley, Portsmouth, Rochdale,
Darlington, Grimsby Town, Workington
(1964-1977).* Solid workman-like defender
who made Pompey his only southern club
when he moved down from Burnley with Fred
Smith as part of a £15,000 double deal. Spent
two years at Fratton Park but turned down the
chance of an additional year to return to his
northern roots. Became a newsagent and did
this for seventeen years. Colin had to undergo
a triple heart by pass and since 1993, has
been working as a school caretaker at a
school where his wife is the Deputy
Headteacher..

BLYTH, Bob

(Manager between 1901 and 1904.)
*Career: Rangers, Preston NE, Portsmouth
(1891-1904).* Played for Pompey at the turn of
the century and later managed the Southern
League championship winning side of 1901-2.
He was manager until 1904 and served the
club as director and chairman. His brother
William and son Robert also played for
Pompey. Blyth died in 1941 at the age of only
41 and is buried in Milton Cemetery, a stone's
throw from the ground.
Bob's sister, Barbara, was Bill Shankly's mum!

BLYTH, Robert

8 apps, 2 goals (1921-1922)
*Career: Portsmouth, Southampton (1921-
1923).* Son of Bob (see above), Robert only
managed eight appearances for Pompey
before taking the short trip 'up the road'.
Unusually for the era, he also played a couple
of matches in the American Soccer League
for the Boston Wonder Workers. Robert died
in 1956.

Jeroen Boere
Photo: Ann Boere

BOERE, Jeroen

5 apps (1994)
Career: *SBV Excelsior, De Graafschap, VVV-Venlo, Go Ahead Eagles, Portsmouth (loan), West Bromwich Albion (loan), Crystal Palace, Southend United, Omiya Ardija (1995-1999).*
A 6ft 4in dutch striker who played five league games on loan from West Ham in 1994. Had to retire from football when he lost an eye, due to a stabbing in Tokyo. He had been playing (and scoring goals) for local club, Omiya Ardija in the Japanese second division. Ran the Half Moon pub in Epping between 1999 and 2004, but died in 2007 at the age of 39 while living in Marbella, Spain.

BOWLER, Gerry

9 apps (1946-1949)
Career: *Derry City, Belfast Distillery, Portsmouth, Hull City, Millwall (1945-1954).*
Northern Ireland international defender who probably joined Pompey at the wrong time because he was competing with so many great players. Was in the squad and played three times during the 1948-49 championship winning season but moved on to Hull after a total of only nine appearances. Died in Crawley in March 2006.

BOWMAN, Tommy

85 apps, 3 goals (1904-1909)
Career: *Blackpool, Aston Villa, Southampton, Portsmouth (1986-1910).* Scottish half back, played for Blackpool, Aston Villa, and 85 games for Pompey before signing for Eastleigh Railway Athletic in 1910. Worked in Southampton docks as a boiler scaler. Died on 27th August 1958 at the age of 84.

BRADBURY, Lee

167 apps, 46 goals (1995-1997 & 1999-2004)
Career: *Portsmouth, Exeter C, Man City, Crystal P, Birmingham C, Portsmouth, Sheff Wed, Derby Co, Walsall, Oxford U, Southend U, Bournemouth (1995-date).* Former soldier, joined Pompey for the first of his two spells at the club in 1995. Was snapped up by Manchester City in July 1997 for £3million, but moved back south very quickly,. His first stop was at Crystal Palace and then back to Fratton Park in 1999. The transfer fee for his return was a tenth of the sum that City had paid less than two years before. Bradders is still playing and is now at Bournemouth.
Player of the season in 1997.

Lee Bradbury. *Back in a Pompey shirt in 2010 for a charity game against Fareham Co-Op.*

BRADY, Garry

14 apps (2001-2002)
Career: *Spurs, Newcastle United, Norwich City, Portsmouth, Dundee, St Mirren (1993-date).* Scotland Under 18 international who was considered to be one of the brightest prospects of his day. His stay in England was less than successful and had to return home to really make his mark. Joined Dundee in 2002 and currently playing for St Mirren.

BRETTELL, Frank

(Manager between 1898 and 1901)
A scouser who managed the club at the turn of the century. During this time he lived in a house called Anfield Cottage in Jubilee Road, Southsea. Although little is know about his life after football, he is still remembered by Plymouth Argyle fans as being one of the key figures in their club's history. As an early manager he helped them form a professional team and win entry into the Southern League.

Became a publican and ran a number of pubs for Whitbreads including the White Hart in Porchester. More recently has worked at Porchester Social Club.

BROWN, Allan

74 apps, 8 goals (1944-1966.)
Career: *Blackpool, Luton Town, Portsmouth, Wigan Athletic (1950-1962).* Wing half who played for East Fife in Scotland before Blackpool tempted him to the Lancashire coast. He joined Pompey in 1961 after a spell at Luton and was part of the team that won the Third Division championship in 1961/2. Later managed a number of clubs including Luton, Bury and most Notably, Nottingham Forest. Returned to the Blackpool area and enjoyed retirement in Lytham St Annes, until his death in March 1996.

BROWN, Arthur

9 apps (1907-1910.)
Career: *Portsmouth, Southampton, (1907-1912).* Went from Pompey's third choice keeper to Great Britain's reserve goalkeeper at the 1912 Olympic Games! Later emigrated to Canada where he worked as a civil engineer.

BRISLEY, Terry

69 apps, 15 goals (1979-1981)
Career: *Leyton Orient, Southend United, Millwall, Charlton Athletic, Portsmouth (1967-1980).* A Londoner who made an immediate impact following his move from Charlton in 1979. From midfield, he scored five goals in his first eight games, which ultimately helped earn promotion from the Fourth Division. He joined Maidstone on a free transfer in 1981 and played the rest of his football for non-league sides. Settled in Brentwood, Essex and worked in the City of London as a Foreign Exchange Broker. Now working as a gardener, mainly for the eldery and loves it.

BROWN, James (Jimmy)

5 apps (1980)
Career: *Aston Villa, Preston NE, Portsmouth, Hibernian (1960-1981).* Ended his career back in Scotland, with Hibernian. Moved back to his native Birmingham where he worked as a sports development officer on the local council for 26 years until taking early retirement.

BROMLEY, Brian

98 apps, 3 goals (1968-1971)
Career: *Bolton Wanderers, Portsmouth, Brighton & H A, Reading, Darlington (1962-1974).* Lancashire born midfielder, joined Pompey in 1968 for £25,000 after eight years with Bolton Wanderers. Later captained Brighton to promotion from the Third Division. Also played for Reading, Darlington and Wigan Athletic before moving back to the area to play for Waterlooville who were managed by his old house-mate David Munks.

BROWN, William

9 apps, 2 goals (1968-1969)
Career: *Southampton, Gillingham, Portsmouth, Brentford (1960-1969).* Bill Brown had earned a reputation as a deadly striker in non-league football and had scored 33 goals in 100 odd games for Gillingham. unfortunately the 6ft 2in striker failed to replicate this success in his time at Fratton Park and he quickly moved on to Brentford. An Ankle injury ended his career and he went back to work on the family's pig farm. He later bought a lorry and started his own conservatory company.

BRYANT, Steve

128 apps, 6 goals (1979-1982)
Career: *Birmingham City, Sheffield Wednesday, Northampton Town, Portsmouth, Northampton Town (1971-1982).* A Londoner who had been Northampton Town's Player of the Year before signing for Pompey in 1979. He returned to the Cobblers after three years of solid performances either in midfield or latterly as a left back. He emigrated to Australia in 1984, where he spent four years playing for Canberrra City whilst working as a sales manager for a dairy firm.

BUCKLE, Harry

15 apps, 3 goals. (1906-1907)
Career: *Sunderland, Portsmouth, Bristol Rovers, Coventry City, Belfast Celtic (1903-1912).* Briefly played for Pompey at the turn of the century and went on to become the first ever manager of Coventry City. Another useless fact - his brother worked in the Belfast dockyard and helped to build the Titanic.

BUICK, Albert

310 apps, 10 goals. (1903-1911)
Career: *Heart of Midlothian, Portsmouth (1902-1911).* 'Spider'(nicknamed because of his dangly arms), died in 1948

BURCHILL, Mark

25 apps, 8 goals (2001-2005)
Career: *Celtic, Birmingham C, Ipswich T, Portsmouth, Dundee, Wigan Ath, Sheff Wed, Rotherham, Hearts, Dunfermline, Kilmarnock. (1997-date).* Arrived at Fratton Park having made a fantastic start to his career at Celtic. He had scored 20 goals in only 17 starts and earned a call up to the Scottish national side. He signed for Pompey in a £600,000 deal but suffered a knee injury after only a couple of games and never fully regained his place in the side. He returned to Scotland and is now with Kilmarnock, who he joined in July 2009.

BURNS, Chris

116 apps, 12 goals (1990-1995)
Career: *Portsmouth, Swansea City, Bournemouth (loan), Northampton Town (1990-1996).* Chris was playing non league football for Cheltenham and working as a bricklayer when offered a trial at Fratton Park. He did enough to earn a contract and played over 100 games for the Blues including the FA Cup semi-final against Liverpool in 1992. He remained in the pro game for another two years before returning to the west country. Had a brief spell as manager of Cinderford Town and later played in Spain for UD Horadada until the owners went bust. Now working with the Under 16's at Cheltenham.

Ex-Pompey pros finally get their hands on the FA Cup.

BURROWS, Frank

(Manager 1979-192 and 1990-1991.)
Career: *Raith Rovers, Scunthorpe United, Swindon Town (1962-1974).*
Frank had enjoyed a twelve year playing career and was a key part of Swindon Town's League Cup winning side of 1969. His first management role was as Jimmy Dickinson's assistant and took over the manager's job when Gentleman Jim resigned in 1979. The team won promotion from the Fourth Division in 1980 but his first spell in charge only lasted until 1982. He then worked as assistant manager at Sunderland before moving back to Wales to take the helm at Cardiff City. Having guided the Welsh club to promotion, he resigned in August 1989 and accepted an invitation to return to Fratton Park as John Gregory's assistant. Became manager again when Gregory left the club but could not reverse a downward trend and was relieved of his duties the following year. He has since coached/managed at Swansea, West Ham (under Harry Redknapp), Cardiff City, and Leicester City where he briefly took over as caretaker manager.

Photo: wjarrettc

BURTON, Deon

87 apps, 17 goals (two spells) (1994-1997 and 2002-2004) Career: *Portsmouth, Cardiff city (loan), Derby County, Barnsley (loan), Stoke City (loan), Portsmouth, Walsall (loan), Swindon Town (loan), Brentford, Rotherham United, Sheffield Wednesday, Charlton Athletic (1994-date).* Only 5ft 8in tall but deadly in the penalty box, not only as a goalscorer but as a creater of opportunities for others. Burton has enjoyed two spells at Fratton Park, the first as an 18 year old finding his feet in the league until a £1 million move took him to Derby County, who were managed by Jim Smith at the time. The second in the early 2000's when he returned for a fee of £75,000 which rose to £250,000 upon promotion. However he failed to secure a regular starting spot and continued on his travels. His most recent club was Charlton Athletic who he joined in 2008 and played for until he agreed a deal to play for Tony Adams at Azerbaijani club Gabala.
Jamaican international and played in the 2008 World Cup.

BUSBY, Martyn

6 apps, 1 goal (on loan) (1975-1976)
Career: *QPR, Portsmouth, Notts County, QPR, Burnley. (1970-1980).* Played a handful of games on loan from QPR in 1976. Younger brother of former Fulham striker Viv Busby. Martyn ran a pub, was briefly manager of Beaconsfield and then joint manager of Maidenhead United with former West Ham player Alan Devonshire.

BUTLER, Ernie

242 apps (1938-1952)
Career: *Portsmouth (1938-1952).*
Became one of the club's greatest ever goalkeepers but had only ended up between the sticks by chance. While playing at left back in a Bath & District League match, the regular keeper received a knock and as the tallest player in the side, Ernie was given the gloves. He played in every match in both of Pompey's Championship winning years and played over 200 league games in total. At the end of his career he stayed in the Portsmouth area to run a fruit and vegetable business and then ran the George & Dragon pub for seventeen years.

BUTTERS, Guy

187 apps, 7 goals (1990-1997)
Career: *Tottenham Hotspur, Southend United (loan), Portsmouth, Oxford United (loan), Gillingham, Brighton & H A, Barnet (loan), Havant & Waterlooville, Lewes, Winchester City (1988-date).* Solid 6ft 2in defender who won three England Under 21 caps while with Tottenham, joined Pompey for £375,000 in September 1990. Over the next six years he clocked up over 180 appearances in all competitions and won over an initially sceptical crowd. Although he still lives in the area now, he moved to Gillingham in 1996 and played out the remainder of his league football with Brighton and Barnet. Lives in Hedge End and pulled on a blue shirt again for an ex-Pompey XI in the summer of 2010.

BUXTON, Lewis

30 apps (2000-2004)
Career: *Portsmouth, Exeter City (loan), Bournemouth (loan), Stoke City, Sheffield Wednesday (2000-date).* Former Pompey youngster, born on the Isle of Wight, Lewis initially moved to Stoke City but signed for Sheffield Wednesday in January 2009 and is still part of their defence today.

CAHILL, Paul

112 apps, 2 goals (1974-1978)
Career: *Coventry City, Portsmouth, Aldershot, Tranmere Rovers, Stockport County (1973-1978).* A Liverpool lad who played most of his League football while at Pompey. Ended his playing days in the USA, where he appeared for California Surf and San Jose Earthquakes. During his time at Fratton Park he battled gamely in a poor side and was named Player of the Year in 1976 and the following season became the club's youngest ever captain at the age of 21.

CAMPBELL, Bobby

68 apps, 3 goals (1961-1966)
Career: *Liverpool, Portsmouth, Aldershot (1958-1967).* Started as a player with Liverpool, but made his name as a manager at Portsmouth (1982-4) and then Chelsea (1988-1991). Bobby's most recent post involved coaching in Saudi Arabia.

CAMPBELL, Sol

111 apps, 2 goals (2006-2009)
Career: *Tottenham Hotspur, Arsenal, Portsmouth, Notts County, Arsenal (1992-date).* Undoubtedly one of the biggest names to pull on a Pompey shirt in recent years. The memory of Sol lifting the FA Cup will live in the memory for many a year, but it is a shame that his relationship with the club ended on such a sour note. Unpaid monies being at the heart of a dispute that led to court in March 2010. Having been given a seemingly unlikely second chance at Arsenal in 2009, he snubbed the chance of an additional year and signed for Newcastle United in August 2010.

CARTER, Brian

44 apps 0 goals ((1956-1960)
Weymouth, portsmouth, Bristol Rovers (1956-1961) Joined Pompey as a 17 year old from Weymouth, in 1956 and played as a forward for three years before moving on to Bristol Rovers. After only four appearances he accepted an offer to play semi-pro for Bath City, where he earned more money and teamed up with fellow ex-Pompey players Pat Neill and Len Phillips. It was there that he began working for a quarry mining company before eventually setting up his own Stone Supplies business.

CARTER, Jimmy

80 apps, 6 goals (1995-1998)
Career: *Millwall, Liverpool, Arsenal, Portsmouth, Millwall (1983-1999).* An exciting winger who looked set for a glittering career in his early days at Millwall where he played in the same team as Teddy Sheringham. Signed for Pompey in 1995, having played only a handful of games for his previous two clubs, Liverpool and Arsenal. Despite only being a squad player at Highbury he did win Championship and FA Cup winners medals. He became Terry Fenwick's first signing but only showed glimpses of his undoubted talent during his two year stay. Having retired from football due to a back injury, Jimmy has invested his money in property and lives in Crieff, Scotland. He has also recently played for the Arsenal side in Sky TV's Masters tournament.

CASEY, Mark

Career: *Celtic, Portsmouth, St Patrick's Athletic (loan), Ayr United, Glenafton Athletic, Albion Rovers, Clyde (1999-2009).* Spent three years at Fratton Park without making a League appearance. Moved back to Scotland where he was sent to prison in November 2008, having been caught driving whilst three times over the limit. Signed for Belshill Athletic in January 2010.

CASEY, Tommy

25 apps, 1 goal (1958-1959)
Career: *Leeds Utd, Bournemouth, Newcastle Utd, Portsmouth, Bristol City (1949-1963).* Won 12 caps with Northern Ireland and played for them in the 1958 World Cup. However,Casey only lasted eight months at Fratton Park before moving on to Bristol City for £5,000 in 1959. coached a number of clubs, becoming trainer-coach at Everton in the late 60s, then chief coach at Coventry City in July 1972. Became manager of Third Division Grimsby Town in February 1975 when the team were in relegation trouble (they finished the season in 16th position). After a promising start to the 1975/76 season Grimsby struggled again, finishing in 18th. Casey left the club in November 1976, but went on to manage other clubs overseas. before his death on 13th January 2009 at the age of 78.

CHADWICK, Arthur

70 apps, 12 goals (1901-1904)
Career: *Burton Swifts, Southampton, Portsmouth, Northampton Town, Accrington Stanley, Exeter City (1985-1912).* Played 70 games for Pompey having moved from Southampton in 1901. Managed Exeter, Reading and Southampton, but died in 1936 while watching a match at Exeter City's ground.

CHALKIAS, Konstantinos

6 apps (2005)
Career: *Apollon Larissa, Panathinaikos, Apollon Athens, Panathinaikos, Iraklis, Panathinaikos, Portsmouth, Real Murcia, Aris Thessaloniki, PAOK (1993-date).* Greek goalkeeper, whose unconvincing performances in 2005 opened the door for Jamie Ashdown to make his Pompey mark. Left after only 5 league appearances. He has since played in Spain and back home in Greece, where he currently is on the books of PAOK.
Has won 27 caps with the Greek national side (so far!)

CHAMBERLAIN, Mark

198 apps, 22 goals (1988-1994)
Career: *Port Vale, Stoke City, Sheffield Wednesday, Portsmouth, Brighton & H A, Exeter City (1978-1998).* A former England international winger who was born in Stoke and made his league debut as a 16 year old for Port Vale. His exciting style earned him a regular first team place and was named by the Star as the Fourth Division's best player in 1981. Local arch rivals, Stoke City, persuaded him to move across the town in 1982 and it was while he was there that he won his eight England caps. Sheffield Wednesday benefited from his skill before he became a £300,000 pre-season signing for Pompey in 1988. He ended his League playing days at Exeter following a spell at Brighton and later became player/manager at Fareham Town. Mark took over as assistant coach of the East Timor national side in April 2008 but was back at Fratton Park in the September as part of the coaching staff. Although he fell victim of the cut backs in October 2009 he still lives locally.

Football,
Inside and Out

Steve with IAN RIDLEY
CLARIDGE
BEYOND THE BOOT CAMPS

CHANNON, Mick

40 apps, 6 goals (1985-1986)
Career: *Southampton, Manchester City, Southampton, Newcastle United, Bristol Rovers, Norwich City, Portsmouth (1965-1986).* Made his league debut for Southampton in 1966 and formed a deadly partnership with Ron Davies. It is ironic that they both later played for the Blues. Mick was brought in by fellow ex-Saint Alan Ball as a 37 year old stop gap while he settled his side. Despite winning 46 England Caps and being one of the top players of his day, he openly admitted that the horses were his first love. He is now based at his West Ibsley stables in Berkshire and known nationally as a very successful racehorse trainer. Can also often be heard commentating on both radio and television.

CHAPMAN, Lee

6 apps, 2 goals (1993)
Career: *12 league clubs including Arsenal, West Ham, and Leeds United (1978-1996).* A well travelled striker who won one cap for the England at under 21 and B level's. Much respected for his scoring record, he joined Pompey on a free transfer from Leeds but quickly moved on to West Ham for £250,000 in September 1993. Quit the game to run a wine bar in Chelsea. Now does media work and is married to the 'Men Behaving Badly' star Leslie Ash. They now live in London and own a number of catering establishments including restaurants and wine bars.

CHAPMAN, Sammy

58 apps, 11 goals (1958-1961)
Career: *Mansfield Town, Portsmouth, Mansfield Town (1956-1963).* An Irish wing half who spent three years at Fratton Park was later banned from football following a bribes scandal. He had been born on same street in Belfast as Derek Dougan and was also at Pompey at the same time as the 'Doog' having first come across the water to serve his apprenticeship at Manchester United After two years with Mansfield Town, he moved back to the south coast and worked as car salesman and then for the Southern Electricity Board. Scouted for Wolves, Leicester and the FA into the early 2000's until his retirement.

CHRISTENSEN, Tommy

4 apps, 2 goals (1986-1987)
Career: *Elche CF, Leicester City, Portsmouth, Brondby IF, Vejle Boldklub, Eintracht Braunschweig (1984-1989).* Later played in Denmark (home country) for Brondby and in Germany for Eintract Braunschweig.

CHRISTOPHE, Jean-Francois

0 apps (2007-2008)
Career: *Portsmouth, Bournemouth (loan), Yeovil Town (loan), Southend United (2007-date).* Joined in 2007 but left for Southend before making a League appearance. Still at Roots Hall and scored their goal of the season in 2008/9.

CISSE, Aliou

28 apps (2004-2006)
Career: *Lille, Sedan, PSG, Montpelier, Birmingham City, Crystal Palace (loan), Portsmouth, Sedan, Nimes Olympique (1994-date).* Probably gained most notoriety off the field, when his transfer from Birmingham City hit the headlines, having been brought into question by the Stevens inquiry. Aliou's most recent club was Nimes Olimpique in 2008/9.

CLARIDGE, Steve

122 apps, 37 goals (1997-2001)
Career: *Fareham Town, Bournemouth, Weymouth, Crystal Palace, Aldershot, Cambridge United, Luton Town, Cambridge United, Birmingham City, Leicester City, Portsmouth (loan), Wolverhampton Wanderers, Portsmouth, Millwall, Weymouth, Brighton & HA, Brentford, Wycombe Wanderers, Millwall, Gillingham, Bradford City, Walsall, Bournemouth. (1983-2007).* Claridge will always be a Pompey boy and not just because he was born in the city. His three spells at the club have earned him legendary status although Pompey is just one of the very long list of clubs that he has given great service. At the end of a colourful and extensive career it was logical that he would try his hand at management. Sadly, for all his experience and passion, he was unable to make sufficient impression at Weymouth, Pompey or Millllwall and is now perfectly at home commentating on the TV and radio. *Player of the season in 1999 and 2000.*

Photo: Runningboards

CLARKE, Colin

108 apps, 27 goals (1990-1993)
Career: *Ipswich Town, Peterborough United, Tranmere Rovers, Bournemouth, Southampton, QPR, Portsmouth (1980-1993).*
Northern Irish international striker who ended his playing career at Pompey in 1993, three years after signing from QPR for a record fee of £450,000. He has since coached in America and Puerto Rica - where he is known as "The General" - and took over as manager of the national team in January 2008.

CLIFFORD, George

175 apps, 0 goals (1924-1930))
Career: *Sutton Junction, Portsmouth Mansfield Town, Ilkeston United (1924-1931)*
Right back who hailed from Derbyshire and cost the club £10 when he signed from Sutton Junction in 1924. Was a member of the side that lost 10-0 at Leicester City and was dropped for the following match. This signalled the end of his stay. After a brief spell with Mansfield he retired from the game and ran a poultry farm. Died in 1964

CLARKE, Ike

131 apps, 58 goals (1947-1952)
Career: *West Bromwich Albion, Portsmouth, Yeovil Town (1937-1952).*
A traditional 'number nine' who had a fantastic eye for goal. He had already proved his worth at West Brom before signing for Pompey as a 37 year old. It only took him six minutes to get his first goal for the club and went on to play throughout both of the Championship winning seasons before hanging up his boots in 1952. He then moved to live in Herne Bay, Kent and helped raise funds for the County Cricket Club.

COLE, Andy

22 apps, 4 goals (2006-2007.)
Career: *Arsenal, Fulham, Bristol City, Newcastle U, Man U, Blackburn Rovers, Fulham, Man City, Portsmouth, Birmingham C Sunderland, Burnley (loan), Nottm Forest (1989-2008).* Prolific goalscorer who played for some of the country's top clubs (including Pompey!). Retired as a player in November 2008. Joined his old Manchester United team mate, Paul Ince, at Milton Keynes Dons as a coach in August 2009. A week later he left the club to help train the strikers at Huddersfield Town, a post that was considerably closer to his home in Alderley Edge, Cheshire.

George Clifford

Andy Cole
Photo: Egghead06

COLLARD, Ian

2 apps (1975-1976)
Career: *West Bromwich Albion, Ipswich Town, Portsmouth (loan) (1964-1975).* Made two starts in a Pompey shirt in the 70's but had been a regular for West Bromwich Albion and Ipswich Town prior to his arrival. He joined briefly on loan from the Suffolk club in 1975/6 but his services were not required and he returned to Portman Road. A hip injury forced him to retire from soccer in 1976, but he continued to be involved with sport, travelling extensively from his home in Bristol. His stops have included Kuwait, New Zealand, America and Australia. Later became a school teacher but was forced to retire due to problems with his hips, which led to the need for surgery.

COLLINS, Eamonn

8 apps (1986-1989)
Career: *Blackpool, Southampton, Portsmouth, Exeter City, Colchester United, Exeter City (1980-1992).* Became the youngest player to ever make an appearance in s professional match in England, when he made his debut for Blackpool, six weeks before his 15th birthday. Alan Ball was a big fan of this Irish midfielder and worked with him at four clubs including Pompey in the 1980's. Eamonn eventually returned to Ireland and went into coaching with his home town club St Patrick's Athletic. He has been a FIFA registered player's agent since 2006.

CONNOR, Terry

58 apps, 14 goals (1987-1990)
Career: *Leeds United, Brighton & H A, Portsmouth, Swansea City, Bristol City (1979-1992).* A £250,000 capture from Brighton, purchased to score goals following Pompey's promotion to the First Division in 1987. A run of injuries kept him out of the side and he was given an escape route by Frank Burrows, who took him to Swansea in a £25,000 deal. Subsequently moved into coaching, initially with Bristol Rovers, and now with Wolves, where he is assistant manager.

COOK, Aaron

1 app (1998-99)
Career: *Portsmouth, Crystal Palace, Havant & Waterlooville (1997).* Joined Eastleigh in October 2009. Aaron was named in the Blue Square South All Stars Team the previous season, while playing for Salisbury.

COOK, Andy

9 apps (1997-1998)
Career: *Southampton, Exeter City, Swansea City, Portsmouth, Millwall (1987-1999).* Now back living in his home town of Romsey and working in sports therapy.

COOPER, Shaun

7 apps (2000-2005)
Career: *Portsmouth, Leyton Orient (loan), Kidderminster Harriers (loan), Bournemouth (2000-date).* Former Pompey youngster joined current club, Bournemouth, in 2005.

CORDJOHN, Barry

17 apps (1964-1965)
Career: *Charlton Athletic, Aldershot, Portsmouth (1960-1964).* Only played 17 games before being released on a free transfer. During a game for Margate, he suffered a gashed leg and a few days later was rushed to hospital with suspected tetanus. It was thought that this may have been something to do with the fact that sheep had grazed on the land during the Second World War. This led to the PFA introducing compulsory tetanus injections for all players. After a short spell working as a set erector for the BBC, Barry became a driver for a wealthy Arab. Now lives in Weybridge and drives for a gentleman in London.

COWAN-HALL, Paris

Youngster who had trials with both Manchester United and Chelsea before signing for Pompey. Was released at the end of the 2009/10 season having failed to break into the first team squad and signed a short term deal with Scunthorpe in October 2010

COX, Freddie

(Manager between 1958 and 1961)
In his playing days, was know as a tricky winger but the second world war interrupted his career. He joined the RAF and won the Distinguished Flying Cross as a fighter pilot. His spell as Pompey manager was not a great success, but he did fare better in charge of Gillingham and Bournemouth following his departure from Fratton Park in 1961. Died in August 1973, he was only 52 at the time.

CRANIE, Martin

5 apps (2007-2009)
Career: *Southampton, Portsmouth, Coventry 2004-date).* England Under 21 defender who followed Harry Redknapp from Southampton.

He had previously been in the same Saints youth team as Gareth Bale and Theo Walcott but has not emulated their success. He was released after only two games for Pompey and joined Coventry City in August 2009.

CRAWFORD, Ray

22 apps, 12 goals (1957-1958)
Career: *Portsmouth, Ipswich Town, Wolverhampton Wanderers, West Bromwich Albion, Ipswich Town, Charlton Athletic, Colchester United (1957-1971).* Mention the name 'Ray Crawford' to any Ipswich Town or Pompey fan of a 'certain age' and you will quickly realise that he is still revered and remembered as one of the greatest forwards of his day. A great goalscorer and England international, Ray was actually born on Fratton Road and so it is fitting that he should play for the club and can be classed as a true 'local hero'. In a career that spanned fourteen years, he bagged over 300 goals, but is probably best remembered nationally for the brace he scored for Colchester United against the mighty Leeds team of the time in the fifth round of the 1970/1 FA Cup. When he retired,

Ray Crawford with Linvoy.

Ray became youth coach at Brighton, briefly working under Brian Clough, and then held a similar post at Fratton Park. At the end of his football career he worked as a representative and merchandiser for Nurdin & Peacock, but is now enjoying a happy retirement in Porchester. His autobiography entitled "Curse of the Jungle Boy" was published in 2007.

CREANEY, Gerry
69 apps, 36 goals (1994-1995)
Career: Celtic, Portsmouth, Manchester City, plus short spells at ten more clubs in England and Scotland. (1987-2000). Retired in December 2000 and is now coaching at Bellshill Athletic FC in Scotland.

CROPLEY, Alex
14 apps, 2 goals (1981- 1982)
Career: Hibernian, Arsenal, Aston Villa, Newcastle United (loan), Portsmouth (1968-1982). Scottish international (3 caps) was lured to London by Arsenal in a £150,000 transfer from Hibernian in 1974 but made a far greater impression after he was transferred to Aston Villa. Cropley arrived at Fratton Park via Toronto Blizzard and at the end of his career, which was cut short by injury after only a few games. Retired in 1983 and ran a pub in Edinburgh. More recently he has been working as a taxi driver in the same city.

Peter Crouch

CROUCH, Peter
88 apps, 35 goals in 2 spells (2001/2 and 2008/9) Career: Tottenham Hotspur, QPR, Portsmouth, Aston Villa, Norwich City (loan), Southampton, Liverpool, Portsmouth, Tottenham Hotspur (1998 - date). Still knocking in the goals for Spurs and England. *Player of the season in 2002.*

CROWE, Jason
93 apps, 5 goals (1999-2003)
Career: Arsenal, Crystal Palace (loan), Portsmouth, Brentford (loan), Grimsby Town, Northampton Town, Leeds United (1996-date). Former Arsenal junior who joined Pompey in 1999 for a £1 million fee. He was instrumental in helping Pompey gain promotion to the Premier League,. Nevertheless, he was one of the first players released by Harry Redknapp to make way for new signings in 2003. Now playing for Leeds United, who he joined in July 2009.

CROWN, David
31 apps, 3 goals (1981-1983)
Career: Brentford, Portsmouth, Exeter City, Reading, Cambridge United, Southend United, Gillingham (1980-1993). A Frank Burrows acquisition after he had impressed as a Brentford player in a match against Pompey. Joined in a straight swap, with Chris Kamara making the move to west London. The form of Alan Rogers meant that Crown spent much of his time on the bench and he eventually moved on to Reading. David qualified as an accountant in 1992 and now runs his own practice in Essex. You can visit his website at: http://www.davidcrownuk.co.uk

Helping to fight testicular cancer!

CUNDY, Jason

11 apps (1999-2000)
Career: *Chelsea, Tottenham Hotspur, Crystal Palace (loan), Bristol City (loan), Ipswich Town, Portsmouth (1988-2000).* Forced to retire due to injury in 2000. Has since worked in the media with talkSport and Chelsea TV. Made the news himself when it was revealed that he had been diagnosed with testicular cancer. Now fully recovered, Jason now lives in Upton Grays and devotes much of his time to a charity that raises awareness of the problem. He earns a living from the media including a phone in with Scott Minto on The Blues in-house television channel, has worked for Sky TV and Talksport Radio also ran an events company with Clive Walker.

CUNLIFFE, Dan.

306 apps, 178 goals. (1899-1900)
Career: *Oldham County, Liverpool, New Brighton, Portsmouth, New Brighton Tower, Portsmouth, New Brompton (Early 1900's).* Scorer of Pompey's first ever goal in the FA Cup proper. Died at Heywood, Lancashire in 1937.

CURTIS, John

7 apps (2004-2005)
Career: *Manchester United, Barnsley, Blackburn Rovers, Sheffield United, Leicester City, Portsmouth, Preston NE, Nottngham Forest, QPR, Wrexham, Northampton Town (1995-date).* Former Manchester United junior who was touted as a bright prospect for the future when he appeared in their FA Youth Cup winning side of 1995. Enjoyed a brief period of success at Blackburn following a £1.5 million move to Ewood Park. His Pompey stay was even shorter and he quickly moved on to Nottingham Forest. John signed for Northampton Town in July 2009 but is now playing for Gold Coast in Australia.

CURTIS, Tom

15 apps (2000-2002)
Career: *Derby County, Chesterfield, Portsmouth, Mansfield Town, Chester City, Notts County (1991- 2008).* Signed by Tony Pulis for £150,000 but he missed more than a season through injury and only made 15 appearances in two years. Has been playing for Conference North side Alfreton Town since 2008.

Dan Cunliffe

Remember the old Milton End... particularly in the rain?

CUTLER, Reg
107 apps, 14 goals (1958-1962)
Career: *WBA, Bournemouth, Portsmouth, Stockport County (1951-1962).* Reg played over 100 games after Freddie Cox snapped him up from Bournemouth in 1958. They had worked together previously at West Brom where Cox had been Assistant Manager. Despite being a deadly penalty taker, Reg never quite managed the step up to the higher division and he was released in 1961. A spell at Stockport County was his last involvement with league football, but he did turn out for a number of non-league sides before retiring completely. He later worked for Oakvale Nurseries in Worcestershire before retiring in 2000. *Once crashed into a goalpost during an FA Cup tie for Bournemouth against Wolves and brought the goal down completely!*

Photo: buster1976

DAISH, Liam
2 apps (1988-1988)
Career: *Portsmouth, Cambridge, Barnet , Birmingham C, Coventry C(1986-2003).* Pompey born, Liam only made one league appearance before leaving to join Cambridge United on a free transfer in 1988. Here he developed into a robust and reliable defender. So much so, that he earned an international call up (Republic of Ireland), and a move to Birmingham City. Later transferred to Coventry City for a £1.5 million fee, but was forced to retire in 1999 due to a knee ligament injury. This did not prevent him from joining up with Havant & Waterlooville, as a player, and for a brief stint as joint manager. Has been manager at Ebsfleet United since 2005 and led them to FA Trophy success in May 2008.

DALE, Gordon
120 apps, 18 goals (1951-1956)
Career: *Chesterfield, Portsmouth, Exeter City, (1948-1960).* A skillful winger who was capable of dazzling dribbling and able to deliver a pinpoint cross. He also possessed a powerful shot and was tipped to play for England. A series of injuries and competition for places limited his chances both at club and international level and he never did make the national side. Gordon played over 100 games for Pompey and ended his professional career at Exeter City. He was then re-united with fellow ex-players Harry Ferrier, Len Phillips, and Mike Barnard at non-league Chelmsford before returning to Portsmouth to take over a newsagents in North End and then a hotel in Southsea. Died in March 1996 at the age of 67.

D'ALESSANDRO, Andres
13 apps, 1 goal (2006 (loan))
Career: *River Plate, Wolfsburg, Portsmouth (loan), Zaragoza, San Lorenzo, Internacional (1998-date).* An exciting Argentinian winger, who won many fans during his brief stay at Fratton Park in 2006. He has been playing for Internacional in his home country since 2008.

Photo: Thiago Piccoli

DANIEL, Ray

122 apps, 5 goals (1990-1995)
Career: *Luton Town, Gillingham, Hull City, Cardiff City, Portsmouth, Notts County, Walsall (1982-1996).* Born in Luton, he began his career with his hometown club Luton Town and later played for Gillingham, Hull City, Cardiff City, Pompey, Notts County and Walsall. He made 90 odd appearances for the Blues between 1990 and 1995 including the FA Cup semi-final against Liverpool in 1992. He was allowed to leave for Walsall on a free transfer in 1995. Later played for North Ferriby and has since coached Hall Road Rangers.

DAVEY, Steve

102 apps, 8 goals (1978-1981)
Career: *Plymouth Argyle, Hereford United, Portsmouth, Exeter City (1966-1982).* Former England youth international, played an integral part in Pompey's promotion from the Fourth Division in 1980. Joined from Hereford United, but he originally hailed from Devon and returned there in 1981 to end his career with Exeter City. Later played for a number of non-league clubs in the area and took over the Chatsworth Rest Home in Plymouth. Can now be heard as a commentator on BBC Radio Devon.

DAVIDSON, Dennis

1 app (1959-1960)
Career: *Torry Rangers, Portsmouth, Andover (1954-1961).* A scotsman who grew up with Denis Law and future Burnley keeper Adam Blacklaw, Davidson signed for Pompey as an amateur in 1954. He made one first team appearance during his six year stay but also took on an engineering apprenticeship with Pompey's chairman of the time, Jack Sparshatt. The offer to open a new branch for Sparshatts in Horsham combined with the chance to earn additional income by playing in the Southern League for Crawley brought his stay at Fratton Park to an end. He later joined British Leyland which included a spell in Nigeria, ran a jewellery business and a pub before settling in Horndean to earn a living buying and selling properties.

DAVIES, John

2 apps (1953-1955)
Career: *Portsmouth, Scunthorpe United, Walsall (1953-1960).* A local lad who had attended the Northern Grammar School made two appearance son the wing in the 1950's but could not dislodge Peter Harris. He later played for Scunthorpe and Walsall before retiring from the game and to join the Police force.

Former players raising money for worthy causes.

DAVIES, Ron

69 apps, 21 goals (1973-1974)
Career: *Chester City, Luton Town, Norwich City, Southampton, Portsmouth, Manchester United, Millwall (loan) (1959-1975).* One of Southampton's all time greatest players, but we will forgive him for that. He moved down the A27 and a couple of divisions to help out at Pompey in 1973. His career seemed to be coming to an end, until, to everyone's surprise, he was signed by Manchester United in November 1974. His stay at Old Trafford was a short one and he returned to the Southampton area before jetting off to the States. He now resides in Albuquerque, New Mexico, works in the construction industry and lives in a motor home.

DAVIS, Sean

116 apps, 4 goals (2006-2009)
Career: *Fulham, Tottenham Hotspur, Portsmouth, Bolton Wanderers (1996-date).* Joined Pompey from Spurs in January 2006 as part of a combined deal that also saw the arrival of Pedro Mendes, and Noe Pamarot. Sean joined Bolton Wanderers in July 2009 on a free transfer, having been the subject of a £3 million bid by the same club, five months earlier, that had been turned down.

Photo: Ben Sutherland

DE ZEEUW, Arjan

118 apps, 5 goals (2002-2005)
Career: *Telstar, Barnsley, Wigan, Portsmouth, Wigan, Coventry City, ADO20 (1992-date).* One of the best free transfers in the club's history. Having already gained League experience with Barnsley and Wigan Athletic, the formidable Dutchman signed for Pompey after his contract with Latics had expired. Was an instant hit on the south coast and played his part in the winning of the First Division Championship. The following year, back in the Premier League, he was named Player of the Year and took over as captain when Teddy Sheringham left for West Ham. It was only a falling out with Alain Perrin that prompted him to move back to his previous club in a £90,000 transfer. Arjan is now back in his homeland and played for ADO'20 until 2009. Since his retirement he has started a new career as a De Zeeuw began working as an investigative detective, specialising in forensics. In a poll to celebrate the centenary of the PFA fans voted De Zeeuw to be Wigan's best player of all time. *Player of the season in 2004.*

DEFOE, Jermain

36 apps, 17 goals (2008-2009.)
Career: *West Ham United, Bournemouth (loan), Tottenham Hotspur, Portsmouth, Tottenham Hotspur (1999-date).* A fantastic goalscorer who, despite such a brief stay, could have still been regarded as a Pompey great, had it not been for his clear disregard for the club and its fans. The way that he handled his departure left a sour taste in the mouth of most supporters. The only small consolation was the £10 'paper' profit made on the purchase and subsequent sale.

Glad to see the back of him?

Lindy Delapenha, then and now.

DELAPENHA, Lindy

8 apps, 1 goal (1948-1950)
Career: *Arsenal, Portsmouth, Middlesbrough, Mansfield Town, Hereford United (1947-1950).* The first Jamaican to play professional football in England. After 380 league games for his three clubs, Lloyd returned to Jamaica and became a popular face as a sports reporter. He worked for the Jamaican Broadcasting Service for over 30 years.

DENYER, Peter

131 apps 15 goals (1975-1978)
Career: *Portsmouth, Northampton T (1975-1982).* Former apprentice who played in a number positions for the first team Moved to Northampton Town for £20,000 in 1979. Later moved 'down under' to coach Blacktown FC.

DERRY, Shaun

55 apps, 1 goal (2000-2002)
Career: *Notts Co, Sheff U, Portsmouth, Crystal P, Notts F (loan), Leeds U, Crystal Palace (1995-2008).* Spent two years at Fratton Park and was captain of the side, before moving to Crystal Palace in 2002 for £400,000. He is now playing for Queens Park Rangers..

DIABATE, Lassina

26 apps (2002-2003.)
Career: *AJ Auxerre, Portsmouth, AC Ajaccio, K Sint-Truidense, V.V., Lausanne Sports, AS Cannes, CS Louhans-Cuiseaux (1992-date).* Fearsome Ivorian defender who can count Pompey as one of his ten clubs, and the only one in the UK. Joined French club CS Louhans-Cuiseaux in January 2009.

DIAO, Salif

13 apps (2005-2006 (loan))
Career: *Liverpool, Birmingham City (loan), Portsmouth (loan), Stoke City (1996-date).* Senegalese midfelder has been with Stoke City since 2007.

DIARRA, Lassana

32 apps, 3 goals (2008-2009)
Career: *Le Havre, Chelsea, Arsenal, Portsmouth, Real Madrid (2003-date).* Probably one of the classiest players to grace Fratton Park and it was no surprise when, in December 2008, Pompey agreed with Real Madrid that he would join them for a fee of around €20 million (£18.88 million). He has since established himself as a first team regular and a fans' favourite.

JIMMY DICKINSON
Portsmouth and England

Young, strong and determined, he is a great team man and had much to do with Portsmouth carrying off the Championship in two successive seasons 1948-50. He has played several times for England without commanding a regular place, a fact which his supporters cannot understand.

DICKINSON, Jimmy

834 apps, 10 goals (1946-1965)
Career: *Portsmouth (1946-1965).* Probably
the most famous Pompey player in the club's
long history. Affectionately known as
'Gentleman Jim', he served the club in almost
every capacity including player, Manager,
Pubic Relations Officer, Club Secretary and
Chief Executive. He made 764 league
appearances for Pompey and won 48 caps for
England, making him the club's most capped
English player of all time. He was awarded
the MBE in 1964 to was named in the list of
100 legends produced to celebrate the
Football League's centenary. Jimmy suffered
three heart attacks , one if which occurred in
a dressing room at Barnsley in 1979. It was
after another in 1982 that he passed away at
the age of 57. The famous 'Pompey Chimes'
rang hauntingly around St Mary's Church in
Fratton at a packed memorial service for the
much-loved legend.
Manager between 1977 and 1979.

DILLON, Kevin

252 apps, 54 goals (1982-1989)
Career: *Birmingham City, Portsmouth,
Newcastle United, Reading (1977-1995).*
Hailed from the north-east but made his
League debut as a Birmingham City player,
having been given the chance by non other
than Sir Alf Ramsey. A £140,000 transfer saw
him arrive at Fratton Park in March 1983
where he instantly became a first team
regular and the club's penalty taker. Over six
years he scored more than his fair share of
goals, many coming from the spot. Dillon was
reunited with his former Birmingham boss Jim
Smith at Newcastle United in 1989 and ended
his career in Berkshire with Reading. He
became coach and then assistant manager at
Elm Park but left the club when Steve Coppell
resigned in May 2009. Was appointed
manager of Aldershot Town in November
2009.

DISTIN, Sylvian

96 apps (2007-2009)
Career: *Newcastle United, Manchester City,
Portsmouth, Everton (1997-date).* After Sol
Campbell's departure, Sylvian was named
club captain. In August 2009, Everton signed
the fans' favourite for a fee of about £5
million.

DOBSON, Tony

66 apps, 3 goals (1993-1997)
Career: *Coventry City, Blackburn Rovers,
Portsmouth, WBA, Gillingham, Northampton
Town (1986-2001).* Dobson joined Pompey
from Blackburn Rovers in September 1993 for
a fee of £150,000 and played in midfield,
central defence and as left back but without
ever managing to establish himself as a first
team regular. After leaving Fratton Park in
1997, he played for West Bromwich Albion,
Gillingham, Northampton Town, and Forest
Green Rovers. Began his second spell as
manager of Southern League side, Rugby
Town in September 2008 but this came to an
end when he resigned in October 2009.

DODSON, Dave

61 apps, 21 goals (1961-1963)
Career: *Arsenal, Swansea City, Portsmouth,
Aldershot, Hereford United (1958-1966).* Ex-
England Youth winger Dave Dodson helped
Pompey clinch the Third Division title in
1961/2. Signing professional for Arsenal in
1957, he failed to secure a first-team slot at
Highbury and joined Swansea before moving
on to Pompey in 1961 for a fee of £4,000. He
later played for Aldershot, Hereford United,
Guildford, Andover and Fleet. Worked as an
estimator for a conservatory company in
Farnborough but is now retired and living in
Barnstaple, Devon.

DOLING, Stuart

52 apps, 5 goals (1991-1994)
Career: *Portsmouth, Torquay United, Doncaster Rovers, Portsmouth (1991-1998).*
A powerful midfielder whose early promise was never fully realised due to a series of injuries and run-ins with successive managers. Doling joined Sydenhams Wessex League's BAT Sports as player/coach in 2003. He also had a short spell as caretaker boss of Lymington & New Milton where he resigned as he couldn't commit enough time to the job.

DORE, Charlie

18 apps (1951-1954)
Career: *Portsmouth (1951-1954).*
Charlie became a goalkeeper by accident! He had previously played as a centre half but in a youth match his team's regular keeper failed to turn up for a game and Charlie was chosen to be his replacement. A Pompey scout spotted his potential and a lengthy playing career followed. Although he only made 18 appearances for the Blues, this number may well have been greater had it not been for National Service. Played non-league football for a number of clubs while working for the Metal Box company, who were his employers for 30 years. When the firm closed down, Charlie opened Kim's Sports in Waterlooville, a shop that he ran for 15 years until he finally retired at the age of 71.

DOUALA, Roudolphe

10 apps (2006-2007)
Career: *St Etienne, Boavista, CD Aves, Sporting CP, Portsmouth (loan), Saint-Etienne, Asteras Tripolis, Plymouth Argyle, Lierse (1997-date).* Cameroonian winger who started his career in France with St Etienne. Later played in Portugal and in England for Pompey and two games for Plymouth Argyle. Now registered with Belgian club, Lierse SK .

DOUGAN, Derek

39 apps, 10 goals (1957-1959)
Career: *Portsmouth, Blackburn Rovers, Aston Villa, Peterborough United, Leicester City, Wolverhampton Wanderers (1957-1976).*
The Doog was spotted by former manager Jack Tinn and joined the club from Belfast Distillery for £4,000 in 1957. Retired from playing in 1975 after playing 532 League games scoring 219 goals, many of them for Wolverhampton Wanderers. At International level he made 43 appearances for Northern Ireland. Dougan was Chairman of the PFA and returned to Molineux in August 1982 as Chairman and Chief Executive. He continued to live in the Wolverhampton area where he worked as a marketing and P.R. consultant. He died on 24th June 2007 aged 69.

DOYLE, Bobby

197 apps, 18 goals (1980-1985)
Career: *Barnsley, Peterborough United, Blackpool, Portsmouth, Hull City (1972-1986).* Joined Pompey from Blackpool in November 1980 and was a member of the team that won the Third Division title in 1983. Injuries forced Bobby to quit after only 43 games for his last club, Hull City. He remained in the area and set up a successful haulage business.

DRINKWATER, Ray

9 apps (1955-1957)
Career: *Portsmouth, Queens Park Rangers, Bath City (1956-1962).* Drinkwater was born in Jarrow, County Durham and began his career with Guildford City F.C. in 1951. He played a handful of games between the sticks for Pompey in the 1956-1957 season but lost his place to Norman Uprichard and signed for QPR in 1957. Went on to play 199 league games for Rangers before leaving Loftus Road in 1963, moving to non league Bath City. He died on the 24 March 2008 aged 76.

DUFFY, Richard

2 apps (2003-2007)
Career: *Swansea City, Portsmouth, Burnley (loan), Coventry (loan), Swansea (loan), Millwall, Exeter City (2001-date).* Very promising Welsh right back was snapped up from Swansea in 2004. However, he never lived up to early expectations despite winning 13 caps for Wales, and was finally released in 2009 after a number of loan spells at clubs in lower divisions. Now playing for Exeter City.

Photo: The Reeds and torkst

DURNIN, John

211 apps, 34 goals (1993-2000)
Career: *Liverpool, WBA(loan), Oxford United, Portsmouth, Blackpool (loan), Carlisle United, Kidderminster Harriers, Rhyl, Port Vale, Accrington Stanley (1986-2004).* 'Johnny Lager' moved to the south coast in 1993, joining from Oxford United for a fee of £200,000. Extremely popular scouser who stayed for seven seasons and scored his fair share of goals. Retired from the game in 2004 after one season with Accrington Stanley. In July 2006, John joined the coaching staff of Southport but left in October of that year. Later coached at Port Vale and then four years at Bolton's Academy. He lives in Warrington, does media work and is a regular for the Liverpool Masters team.

Goal!

EAMES, Billy
18 apps, 3 goals (1975-1977)
Career: *Portsmouth, Brentford (1975-1978).*
Billy Eames played in the same youth team as
Steve Foster and Chris Kamara and scored on
his League debut against Leicester City.
When it became clear that he was unlikely to
secure a regular starting spot he agreed to
join Brentford. Later played for Waterlooville
and studied in London to become a teacher.
Now working at Cams Hall School in Fareham
and has been described by a pupil as "best
teacher eva" on the Rate My Teacher website.

EARL, Stan
0 apps (1950s)
Blond keeper who played non-league football
but had started his career as a junior at
Pompey. Stan has lived in Australia since
2002, where he has become known as a bit of
a 'crooner', often singing alongside Frank
Haffey who was infamous for being the
Scotland goalkeeper who let in nine goals
against England in 1961.

EASSON, Jimmy
312 apps, 107 goals (1928-1938)
Career: *Portsmouth, Fulham (1928-1938).*
Won three caps for Scotland despite attracting
the attention of the England selectors. Played
most of his football for Pompey and was a
regular goalscorer during his ten year stay.
He made three appearances for Fulham
towards the end of his career before returning
to Fratton Park as a trainer. Died in May 1983.

EDINBURGH, Justin
38 apps, 1 goal (1999-2001)
Career: *Southend United, Tottenham Hotspur,
Portsmouth (1988-2002).* Edinburgh left
Spurs for Pompey in 2000 for a fee of
£175,000, playing 35 league games over the
next two years, before joining non-league
Billericay Town as player-manager in July
2003. He had not played a single competitive
game during the Division One title winning
campaign (2002/03). He has since managed
Fisher Athletic, Grays Athletic, and has been
in the hot seat at Rushden & Diamonds since
April 2009.
*Justin was a coach in the football reality TV
show "Football Saved My Life", along with
Neil Ruddock*

EDMUNDS, Redvern
5 apps (1960-1961)
Career: *Portsmouth, Newport County (1960-
1966).* Welshman who returned home after a
single year in the first team squad at Fratton
Park. He had signed on as a member of the
groundstaff at the age of 15 but despite
making his debut as a 17 year old could not
break into the first team on a regular basis.
He later played for some magnificently
named teams: Abergavenny Thursdays;
Latrobe; and Brisbane Hakoah.

EDWARDS, Dennis
80 apps, 16 goals (1964-1967)
Career: *Wycombe Wanderers, Charlton
Athletic, Portsmouth, Brentford, Aldershot
(1958-1967).* Spotted as an amateur playing
for Wycombe Wanderers and had been
capped twice at international level by the time
he signed pro terms with Charlton Athletic.
His career at Pompey started when he moved
from Charlton in January 1965 but his
appearances were limited by injury and he
was loaned to Brentford before signing for
Aldershot on a permanent basis in December
1967. He returned to the Portsmouth area and
started his own successful frozen foods
business. Settled in Denmead and is a keen
golfer.

EDWARDS, Moses
Moses only played one game for Pompey and
died in 1958, but I couldn't resist including
him here because had such a great name!

Jimmy Easson

Len Phillips and Fred Evans

EKNER, Dan

5 apps (1949-1950)
Career: *Portsmouth, Olympique de Marseille, Fiorentina, Chicago Vikings, Atletico Madrid, Rot-Weiss Essen, PSV Eindhoven, Orgryte IS, Vastra Frolunda IF (1945-1963).* Dan Ekner made history when he started his first game for Pompey. By making his debut, he became the first Swedish footballer to play in the English League. Later played in France, Italy, America, Germany, Holland, and finally back in Denmark. Died in his home town of Gothenburg, Sweden in April 1975 at the age of 48.

ELLIS, Peter

278 apps, 2 goals (1973-1984)
Career: *Portsmouth, Southend United, Havant Town (1973-1984).* Attended Southern Grammar School and had thought about becoming a P.E. teacher before being offered the chance to join Pompey. Signed a professional contract in 1974 and became one of the club's most loyal and popular servants. A ten year career saw him play in a variety of positions and for six different managers. The club was relegated twice and also promoted back up to the Third and then Second Division with Ellis in the side. Hung up his boots after spells with Southend United and Havant. Later became a deep sea diver but now works as a fireman based at Southsea Fire Station.

EVANS, Fred

11 apps, 3 goals (1946-1947)
Career: *Portsmouth, Notts County, Crystal Palace, Rochdale, Biggleswade Ton (1946-1953).* Only played 11 games after the Second World War but had been a regular in the side during the hostilities. He remembers making his debut surrounded by a host of famous names who had been recruited as guest players. Later played for Notts County, alongside Tommy Lawton and ended at non-league Biggleswade Town where he became player-manager. Upon his return to the south coast, Fred took a job as Trainee Manager for Brickwoods in Marmion Road, Southsea, and then managed an outlet in Lee-on the-Solent. Retired and still living locally, Fred is involved with and regularly attends functions organised by the ex-pros association.

FAYE, Amdy

52 apps (2003-2005)
Career: *Auxerre, Portsmouth, Newcastle United, Charlton Athletic, Rangers (loan), Stoke City (1998-date).* Senegalese defensive midfielder who started his career in France. Joined Pompey for £1.5 million in August 2003. Injuries restricted his appearances in a blue shirt and he moved on to Newcastle United in January 2005. The transfer later became the subject of a criminal investigation. He was arrested by the City of London police along with Harry Redknapp, Peter Storrie and Willie McKay over allegations of corruption. No charges were ever brought against him and he has since played for Charlton, Rangers, Stoke City and is has been with Leeds United since September 2010..

FENWICK, Terry

(Manager between February 1995 and January 1998.) Had the best part of three seasons as manager but apart from narrowly missing promotion in his second term, success eluded him. Later took over at Northampton Town, Southall and then as Director of Football at Ryman League side Ashford Town. He has since managed a league winning club in the unlikely setting of the Caribbean islands of Trinidad & Tobago, where he is now head coach for San Juan Jabloteh in the Trinidad & Tobago Professional League.

FERNANDES, Manuel

12 apps, 1 goal (2006-2007)
Career: *Benfica, Portsmouth (loan), Everton (loan), Valencia, Everton (loan), Valencia (2004-2008).* Born in Lisbon, Portugal, and initially caught the eye in the colours of Benfica. The plan was for this stylish midfielder to join Pompey for £7 million once a niggling groin injury cleared up. Although he did sign on loan and played a handful of games, by the time his fitness had been proven, it transpired that the fee had escalated to £12 million and would have to be paid if he played three consecutive games. As a result he returned to Benfica. He has since had two spells on loan at Everton but is currently playing in Spain, for Valencia. There was a hope that he would return to Fratton Park in January 2010, but the paperwork was not cleared in time.

FERRIER, Harry

259 apps, 9 goals (1946-1952)
Career: *Portsmouth (1946-1954).*
Pompey was the Scottish full back's only League club although he did manage to play for many of the London based teams while he was stationed at Woolwich during the war. Played over 200 games and enjoyed a spell as captain before he retired in 1954. He later became Gloucester City manager and then spent ten years in charge of Chelmsford City where he won the Southern league Cup four times. Worked in Hoffman's Ball Bearing factory in Essex before retiring. He then took up Bowls becoming a Club and County level player.

FESTA, Gianluca

29 apps, 1 goal (2002-2003)
Career: *Cagliari, Inter Milan, AS Roma, Inter Milan, Middlesbrough, Portsmouth, Cagliari, Nuorese, Tavolara, Sanluri (1986-date).* A tough defender who had played for some of Europe's top teams (and Middlesbough) before adding some steel to the Pompey defence in 2002. His stay was relatively short and he returned home to Italy the following year. Most recently, he signed for Sanluri in 2008, despite being almost 40 years of age. *Interestingly, he had been a martial arts instructor and a junior Italian tennis champion in his younger days.*

Old meets new but which is which?

Harry Ferrier and Jack Froggatt

ARSENAL F.C. OFFICIAL PROGRAMME

PORTSMOUTH PERSONALITIES

STEPHEN

BUTLER

FERRIER

SCOULAR

FROGGATT

DICKINSON

HARRIS

FLEWIN

GAILLARD

REID

CLARKE

PHILLIPS

Pictures by courtesy of "The Evening News," Portsmouth.

FILLERY, Mike

83 apps, 6 goals (1987-1991)
Career: *Chelsea, Queens Park Rangers, Portsmouth, Oldham Athletic (1978-1992).* Strong former Chelsea apprentice, joined the club on a free transfer from QPR in 1987 although he could have been wearing a Pompey shirt four years before if Chairman John Gregory had agreed to the fee demanded by Chelsea supremo Ken Bates. When he did finally arrive he showed glimpses of his ability but was not a regular starter for any of his seasons on the south coast. Frank Burrows eventually sold him to Oldham Athletic for £30,000, but an injury sustained 20 minutes into his debut meant that his career very quickly came to an end. Became assistant manager of BHL League side Crawley Town until August 1994 and then a TV presenter/pundit with Channel East. He has also appeared on Chelsea TV whilst working as a school maintenance manager based in north London.

FLAHAVON, Aaron

104 apps (1996-2000)
Career: *Portsmouth (1994-2001).* Died in a car accident near Bournemouth on 5th August 2001, he was only 25. Aaron suffered from narcolepsy and twice had blackouts during matches. His younger brother Darryl, also a successful keeper, now with Pompey, named his son Aaron in his brother's memory.

FLEWIN, Reg

169 apps (1938-1954)
Career: *Portsmouth (1937-1953).* Pompey born and bred, Reg was a central defender who signed for his home town club on his 17th Birthday in 1937. His career was disturbed by the outbreak of the war when he joined the Royal Marines. Following his playing career Flewin moved into coaching, first taking charge of Pompey's youth team, and later became assistant to manager Eddie Lever. He remained assistant manager until 1960, when he accepted the job as manager of Stockport County. In 1963, he moved back south to become manager at Bournemouth. Reg settled on the Isle of Wight, where he managed the Fort Warden holiday camp in Totland Bay. He died in Shanklin on 24th May 2008, aged 87.

FOGGO, Ken

62 apps, 3 goals (1972-1975)
Career: *West Bromwich Albion, Norwich City, Portsmouth, Brentford (loan), Southend United (1962-1975).* Scottish striker who had enjoyed great success at Norwich City and was their top scorer for three years before the Norfolk club accepted a bid of £25,000 to take him to Fratton Park. Unfortunately the goals dried up and in his two and a half seasons he only added three to his tally. Finished up at Southend in 1976, before ending his playing days at non-league Chelmsford City. Went on to set up a launderette with Bobby Kellard and when their partnership split up he continued in the business running his own launderette and dry cleaners in Chingford, Essex.

FOLEY, Terry

7 apps (1959-1960)
Career: *Portsmouth, Chesterfield (1959-1960).* Portsmouth born and Kingston Secondary School boy, Foley signed for his hometown club from Ryde in January 1959 and featured in seven matches during the 1959/60 season. He later trained as a carpenter's apprentice while playing part time for Yeovil Town who were managed by Basil Hayward at the time. Returned to work in the area and gained employment in his new found trade working for Havant Borough until his retirement.

FOSTER, Craig

18 apps, 4 goals (1997-1998)
Career: *Portsmouth, Crystal, Palace, Northern Spirit (Australia) (1989-2003).* Australian international who may well have stayed longer had it not been for the fact that the club was in administration and had to reduce their wage bill (sound familiar?). As one of the higher earners he was allowed to join Crystal Palace on a free transfer. He played in south London until 2000 when he returned home to Oz. Payed out the rest of his career with Northern Spirit FC before retiring in 2003. Foster is now a commentator for the Special Broadcasting Service but still plays amateur football for Sydney University FC.

FOSTER, Steve

127 apps, 8 goals (1975-1979)
Career: *Portsmouth, Brighton, Aston Villa, Luton Town, Oxford United, Brighton. (1975-1996).* Ian St john's decision to try 'Fozzie' in defence during a reserve game proved to be a key moment in the portsmouth born players career. Although he had scored goals regularly as a youngster, he immediately looked comfortable in te centre half position. Despite the club's poor form and subsequent relegation, Steve 's performances stood out and ultimately earned a £130,000 move to Brighton who had just been promoted to the old First Division. Although he had to go through the agony of relegation at his new club he did win three England caps and captained his side in an FA Cup final replay against Manchester United. With a growing reputation, the fans' favourite was sold to Aston Villa and later played for Luton Town and Oxford United before ending his career

back at the Goldstone Ground. He still lives in the area and runs an extremely successful insurance business offering cover to professional footballers. At any one time they have about 4,000 of the top UK and European players on their books.

Photo: Camw

FOXE, Hayden

46 apps, 2 goals (2002-2004)
Career: *Blacktown City, Ajax, Sanfrecce Hiroshima, KV Mechelen, West Ham United, Portsmouth, Leeds United, Perth Glory, Sydney FC (1994-2010).* Aussie defender who started playing in Sydney before taking his boots on a world tour. His career took in stops at Dutch giants Ajax and the Japanese A-League before West Ham tempted him to these shores. He struggled to adapt to the pace of the Premiership and was given a free transfer after only 12 games. Harry Redknapp had also recently left the club and persuaded the Australian international to join him on the south coast. Became a first team regular and was an integral part of the side that won the First Division title in 2002/3. A bone fracture in his foot the following year sabotaged his run and kept him out of the game for the next season and a half. During this time Alain Perrin had taken over as boss and chose not to renew his expired contract. Returned home to Australia in 2007. Now on the books of his hometown club Sydney FC.

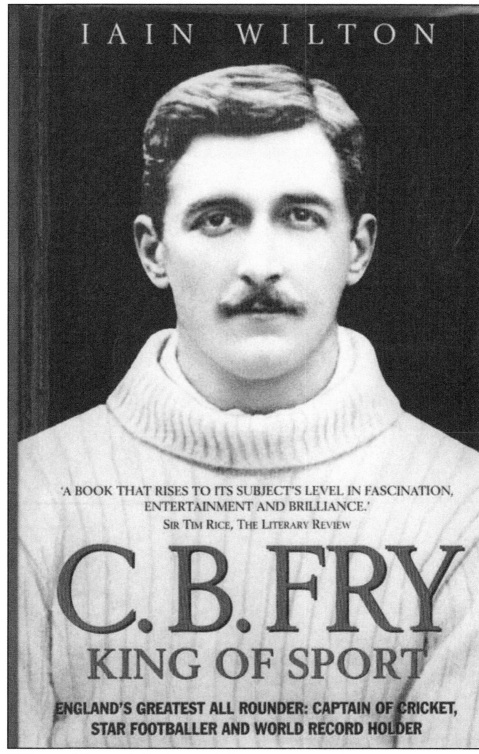

IAIN WILTON

'A BOOK THAT RISES TO ITS SUBJECT'S LEVEL IN FASCINATION, ENTERTAINMENT AND BRILLIANCE.'
SIR TIM RICE, THE LITERARY REVIEW

C.B. FRY
KING OF SPORT

ENGLAND'S GREATEST ALL ROUNDER: CAPTAIN OF CRICKET, STAR FOOTBALLER AND WORLD RECORD HOLDER

CB Fry - read his remarkable story overleaf

Jack Frogatt

FRANCIS, Gerry

4 apps (1984-1985)
Career: *QPR, Crystal Palace, QPR, Coventry City, Exeter City, Swansea City, Portsmouth, Bristol Rovers (1968-1987).* Former England captain who had his best days playing for QPR and Crystal Palace. He joined Pompey briefly at the request of his old England team mate Alan Ball but only made a few appearances before ending his career at Bristol Rovers. He then succeeded Bobby Gould as the Pirates' manager and led the club to promotion out of the Third Division in the following year. This was to be the start of a successful management career with QPR (twice), Tottenham Hotspur and a return to Bristol Rovers. He is now first team coach at Stoke City but also owned his own Antiques business in Chertsey, Surrey.

FROGGATT, Jack

305 apps, 72 goals (1946-1954)
Career: *Portsmouth, Leicester City (1946-1957).* It was natural that Froggatt became a footballer as both his cousin and uncle had player professionally. He first came to Pompey's attention while still in the RAF and working in his father's butchers shop in Commercial Road. Was given his first team debut in 1945. Originally signed as a centre half, he asked the manager for the chance to show what he could do on the wing and seized the opportunity with both hands. This led to over 300 appearances, plenty of goals and international recognition. By the time he reluctantly left the club in 1953 to join Leicester City he had won 13 England caps. He returned to the city almost ten years later

CB Fry *An English Heritage blue plaque can be seen at his birthplace: 144 St James's Road in Croydon*

when his playing career had come to an end and spent the next 22 years as a landlord of the Manor House in Cosham, the Milton Arms around the corner from Fratton Park and latterly the Green Man in Partridge Green, West Sussex. He died at the age of 70 on 17th February 1993.

FRY, C.B.

3 apps (1902-1903)
Career: *Southampton, Portsmouth (1900-1903).* The story of C.B. Fry sounds almost unbelievable and better suited to a TV drama series than a book about former footballers. He lived in the early 1900's and earns his place on the pages by virtue of three games in a Pompey shirt, the third of which was due to be his last ever match due to injury. Apart from his brief footballing career, he was also a sportsman, politician, diplomat, academic, teacher, writer, editor and publisher, and first class cricketer. He played for both the England international football and cricket sides, played in an FA Cup final for Southampton and equalled the world record for the long jump. If that was not enough he also stood as an independent candidate in the General Election and was reputedly offered the chance to take over the throne in Albania. He later launched and edited two magazines for boys, C.B. Fry's Magazine and The Captain, and then started a career in broadcasting. In the late 1920s, he had a breakdown and became paranoid. For the rest of his life, he dressed in bizarrely unconventional clothes and was occasionally seen running stark naked down Brighton Beach. This remarkable man died on 7th September 1956 aged 84.

FULLER, Ricardo

37 apps, 1 goal (2004-2005)
Career: *Crystal Palace, Hearts (loan), Preston North End, Portsmouth, Southampton, Ipswich Town (loan), Stoke City (2001-date).* Jamaican international striker who joined Pompey on a pay-as-you-play deal in 2004. He struggled to find the net and Alain Perrin was happy to let him re-join Harry Redknapp who had since moved on to Southampton. The fee of only £90,000 reflected his value at the time and gave no clue to the fact that he would become a feared Premiership striker in future years. Fuller joined his current club, Stoke City in *2006.*

GAILLARD, Marcel

66 apps, 13 goals (1950-1953)
Career: *Olympique, Crystal Palace, Portsmouth (1947-1952).* Having been the first non-British footballer to play for Crystal Palace, this Belgian winger enjoyed two years at Pompey before dropping down into non-league football. Died in Belgium in 1977.

GALE, Shaun

4 apps (1988-1991)
Career: *Portsmouth, Barnet, Exeter City (1988-2000).* Former Pompey youth player who found his route to the first team blocked by Warren Neil and was restricted to only four appearances before moving away in search of regular football. Barnet gave him that chance and he played 130 games over the next three seasons. In June 1997 a £10,000 transfer took him to Exeter City where his career eventually came to an end. He then joined Havant & Waterlooville as a player and then assistant boss to Dave Leworthy and subsequently Ian Baird. He took full managerial control in October 2007 when Baird accepted a similar role at local rivals Eastleigh. Outside the game he also set up a business in Southampton which supplied workwear and embroidered clothing.

GAMBLIN, Derek

1app, 0 goals (1965-1966)
Career: *Olympique, Crystal Palace, Portsmouth (1947-1952).* Only made one League appearance and that was as an amateur for Pompey on the last day of the 1965/6 season. However, he did play for many of the top non-league clubs of the day and was a regular for the England and Great Britain amateur sides. Worked in the family business, Meon Valley Nurseries but he has also turned out for the Pompey ex-pros XI.

GARNER, Alan

44 apps, 3 goals (1979-1981)
Career: *Millwall, Luton Town, Watford, Portsmouth, Barnet (1969-1982).* A Frank Burrows purchase who was heralded as "as good a player as we are likely to get". He certainly impressed in the heart of the defence before being released on a free transfer when Bobby Campbell took over as manager. Finished his career at non-league Barnet and was a director of a double glazing firm in Hitchin. The company was wound up in 2008 but Alan still regularly attends Luton's games and at one time had an executive box at Kenilworth Road.

GARWOOD, Colin

78 apps, 34 goals (1977-1980)
Career: *Peterborough United, Oldham Athletic, Huddersfield Town, Colchester United, Portsmouth, Aldershot (1967-1981).* A prolific goalscorer for all his clubs and added to his tally during his three year stay at Fratton Park. He was initially brought in to replace the popular David Kemp and had to work hard to win the fans over. A goal average of one in every two games for two consecutive seasons helped him achieve this, but it still did not stop him being cast aside by John Deacon. Despite ending up as top scorer in the 1979-80 promotion, Colin moved to Aldershot in the January for £54,000. He now lives in Newark, Notts and works for an engineering company in Wisbech.

GEKAS, Theofanis

1 app (2008-2009)
Career: *Larissa, Kallithea, Panathinikos, Bochum (loan), Bayer Leverkusen, Portsmouth, Hertha Berlin (1998-date).*
A Greek goalscorer who had been top scorer in both Greece and Germany but was never really given a chance to show what he could do at Fratton Park. He had been brought in from German football by Tony Adams but his successor Paul Hart was reluctant to give the Greek a start. Gekas only managed one substitute appearance (which lasted less than a minute) before being released in May 2009. He returned to Bayer Leverkusen who have since lent him to German rivals Hertha Berlin. *Played for Greece in the 2010 World Cup.*

GILBERT, Billy

163 apps (1984-1989)
Career: *Crystal Palace, Portsmouth,*
Colchester United, Maidstone. (1977-1990).
A member of the Crystal Palace 'Team of the
Eighties' and a regular England Under 23
international. Joined Pompey in June 1984 for
£100,000 and formed a successful defensive
partnership with Noel Blake which was
instrumental in breaking the record for letting
in the fewest number of goals in a season,
with only 28 being conceded in 1986/7. After
spells with Colchester and Maidstone, Gilbert
linked up with former Palace and Pompey
team-mate Vince Hilaire at Havant &
Waterlooville, where for a time the pair
became joint managers. Has since bought
and sold second hand cars, worked as a
corporate entertainer at Portsmouth did some
work as a painter and decorator, and is now
into property developing. Lives in Old
Portsmouth.

GILCHRIST, Paul

42 apps, 4 goals (1976-1979)
Career: *Charlton Athletic, Doncaster Rovers,*
Southampton, Portsmouth, Swindon Town,
Hereford United (1969-1979).

Theofanis Gekas
Photo: Andreas Nowak

Essex born Gilchrist was a member of
Southampton's 1976 FA Cup winning side but
this probably contributed to his inability to
settle at Fratton Park. With the crowd turning
on him at every opportunity even though the
whole team was struggling at the time, he was
probably relieved when Swindon Town gave
him an escape route at the end of the 1977-8
season. He later ran a health and fitness club
in the Wiltshire town, but now works for
B.M.W. in Redhill, Sussex as a service advisor
and lives in a village close to Tunbridge
Wells.

GILFILLAN, John

33 apps (1928-1935)
Inverkeithing United, Heart, East Fife,
Portsmouth, QPR. Pompeys' keeper in the
1939 FA Cup final winning side. Died in St
Mary's Hospital, in 1976. He was grandfather
to Southampton's Steve Mills.

GILL, Mervyn

9 apps (1953-1954)
Career: *Portsmouth, Southampton, Torquay*
United (1953-1962). Goalkeeper who spent
most of his playing career with Torquay
United. He had been at Pompey in the early
1950's but had to compete with Norman
Uprichard for a starting place and returned
home to Devon in 1954. Mervyn worked for
English China Clays, from December 1962
until December 1990, when he retired to live
in Bridport, Dorset.

John Gilfallen

GILLIGAN, Jimmy

34 apps, 5 goals (1989-1990)
Career: *Watford, Lincoln City, Grimsby Town, Swindon Town, Lincoln City, Cardiff City, Portsmouth, Swansea City (1981-1993).* Followed Frank Burrows from Cardiff in 1989, when his former boss took up the role of Assistant Manager to John Gregory. He joined for £215,000 but only stayed for a year before going back to Wales to play for Swansea City. Jimmy was forced to retire due to injury in 1993 and has since worked for a number of clubs including Watford, Wimbledon, MK Dons, Boreham Wood, Waltham Forest, Thurrock as well as the PFA. He now scouts for the England U21 team and runs a sports programme at a schools academy.

GITTENS, Jon

98 apps, 2 goals (1993-1996)
Career: *Southampton, Swindon Town, Southampton, Middlesbrough, Portsmouth, Torquay United, Exeter City. (1985-2000).* Another former Southampton player who despite two spells at the Dell, actually signed for Pompey from Middlesbrough. Jim Smith snapped him up on a free transfer and played him in almost every game for two years but when Terry Fenwick took over as boss, Gittens's chances became limited and he agreed to join Torquay United in 1996. Five years later he was back in the area, coaching with Fareham and was famously 'sent off' for calling the linesman a "chicken nugget". He has since coached the Solent University side Team Solent and managed Wessex League Division 1 team, Blackfield & Langley. He now does some coaching for the Hampshire FA.

GLASS, Jimmy

3 apps (1994-1995)
Career: *Crystal Palace, Portsmouth (loan), Gillingham (loan), Burnley (loan), Bournemouth, Swindon Town, Carlisle United (loan), Cambridge United, Brentford, Oxford United (1991-2001).* Jimmy Glass is best remembered for being the goalkeeper who scored the last-minute goal which kept Carlisle United in the Football League in 1999. In a ten year league career, he played for ten different clubs, including a three game loan spell at Pompey. He was drafted in by

Terry Fenwick to fill the gap left by Alan Knight's suspension and an injury to his understudy, Mart Poom. Glass retired from professional football at the age of 27, and found a job as an IT salesman. He later became a taxi driver in Dorset. He lives in the Dorset village of Lytchett Matravers, with his wife, Louise, and their twins and runs a taxi business in the nearby town of Wimborne Minster.

GOLAC, Ivan

8 apps (1984-1985)
Career: *Southampton, Bournemouth, Manchester City, Southampton, Portsmouth (1978-1984).* Born in Croatia, managed Torquay and Dundee United with whom he won the Scottish Cup, as well as teams in Yugoslavia, Serbia, Iceland and the Ukraine. Ran a chocolate factory in Belgrade for a number of years and worked as a technical director for the Libyan FA, now spends most of his time in Vienna. The Yugoslav International, who played eight games on loan for Pompey in the 1980's, was in the news in May 2010 when he put his name forward as a potential candidate for the vacant manager's position at Celtic.

GORDON, Johnny

489 apps, 119 goals (1952-1967)
Career: *Portsmouth, Birmingham City, Portsmouth (1951-1966)*. A Pompey legend, Johnny Gordon was born in the city but was actually registered as a Hibernian player when his hometown club came knocking. His father was in the Navy and based in Scotland at the time but this did not stop the 18 year old agreeing to a move. Made his debut in 1951 against a Blackpool side that contained Mortensen and Matthews and went on to make the number 8 shirt his own. In total he played for over 15 years with only a brief spell at Birmingham interrupting up a fantastic Pompey career. By the time Johnny retired in 1968 he had notched up over 400 appearances. In the sixties he came runner-up in a televised talent show as a singer but chose a career in the licence trade. Ran a number of local pubs and bars living in Southsea until his death on 26th May 2001 aged 69.

GOSNEY, Andy

62 apps (1981-1992)
Career: *Portsmouth, York City, Birmingham City, Exeter City (1981-1993)*. Gosney was born in Southampton but joined Pompey apprentice in 1979. He turned professional in 1981, but lived in the shadow of Alan Knight, making only 62 appearances in thirteen years. Brief spells at Birmingham and Exeter followed before retiring from the game in 1993. *Gosney was credited with giving Darren Anderton the nickname "Sicknote"*

Alex Govan

GOVAN, Alex

12 apps, 2 goals (1957-1958)
Career: *Plymouth Argyle, Birmingham City, Portsmouth, Plymouth Argyle (1946-1960)*. Scottish winger who played over 300 League games in a 13 year career but only 12 of them in a Pompey shirt. He spent six months at Fratton Park during the 1957/8 season but never settled and moved back to Plymouth Argyle where he had enjoyed much more success. In his second spell, he helped the club win the Third Division championship before retiring. He settled in Plymouth and has run a pub, managed Truro City, run a grocer's shop and worked in the tool room for a motor bike parts firm.

GRAHAM, George

71 apps, 6 goals (1974-1977)
Career: *Aston Villa, Chelsea, Arsenal, Manchester United, Portsmouth, Crystal Palace (1962-1977)*. 'Stroller', whose potential was initially spotted by ex-Pompey player Jimmy Easson, went on to enjoy phenomenal success both as a player and manager at Arsenal. He joined Pompey from Manchester United in the twilight of his career as part of a straight swap that took Ron Davies to Old Trafford. He lived in Southsea and provided a calm influence and an experienced head to a struggling side. He could not help prevent relegation to the Third Division in 1975/6 and was used as bait to lure David Kemp to Fratton Park from Crystal Palace as part of the re-building process. His playing days drew to a close after a summer in America with California Surf. He coached various clubs before taking charge of Millwall. Later moved back to Arsenal with great success before accepting an 'unsolicited gift' from Norwegian agent Rune Hauge and was sacked. Has since managed Leeds and Spurs but is now a media pundit.

GREGORY, David

86 apps, 21 goals (1979-1982)
Career: *Peterborough, Stoke City, Blackburn Rovers, Bury, Portsmouth. Wrexham, Peterborough United (1973-1986).* frank Burrows paid Bury £100,000 to add Gregory to his side which was fighting to get out of the Fourth Division. He made an immediate impact, scoring three goals in his first four

games, but the goals dried up and it was with some relief that promotion was finally achieved on goal difference. The following season saw him play in 42 matches and score 12 goals. A change of manager in 1981 led to Bobby Campbell shuffling the team and Gregory was allowed to leave. He joined Wrexham but ended his career where it started, back in Peterborough. He now lives in Lincolnshire and works as a self employed ceramic tiler.

GREGORY, John

(Manager June 1989 -January 1990)
Career: *Northampton Town, Aston Villa, Brighton & H A, Queens Park Rangers, Derby County, Portsmouth, Plymouth Argyle, Bolton Wanderers (1972-1989).* After a successful playing career, the former England midfielder came to Pompey as a 34 year old to work as Alan Ball's assistant. but became manager in his own right in January 1989. His tenure was to last almost exactly one year before going on to take charge at Plymouth, Wycombe, Aston Villa, Derby, and QPR. He managed Israel's top Arab club Maccabi Ahl Nazareth between December 2009 and May 2010 when took over at F.C. Ashdod, also in Israel's top flight.

GRIFFIN, Andy

49 apps (2004-2006)
Career: *Stoke City, Newcastle United, Portsmouth, Derby County, Stoke City, Reading (loan) (1996-date).* Despite having joined Newcastle United for £1.5 million, Pompey managed to pick him up on a free transfer in 2004. Two years later, it was clear that he did not feature in Harry Redknapp's plans and the left back returned to his first club Stoke City. Played Premiership soccer for the Potters but agreed a loan to Reading in January 2010 and signed a permanent deal in the following August. *Photo: TuborgLight*

George Graham & Terry Venables

GRIFFITHS, Carl

16 apps, 2 goals (1995-1996)
Career: *Shrewsbury Town, Manchester City, Portsmouth, Peterborough United, Leyton Orient, Wrexham (loan), Port Vale, Leyton Orient, Luton Town (1988-2007).* Griffiths arrived at Fratton Park as part of the deal that took Kit Symons to Manchester City. He only made two starts during his stay but was a regularly used substitute and scored two goals before moving on to Peterborough United. Later in his career he re-discovered his goalscoring form and achieved cult status at Leyton Orient. Went on to manage Brentwood Town and was later appointed assistant manager at Barkingside of the Essex Senior Football League.

GROVES, Arthur

80 apps, 13 goals (1935-1939)
Career: *Halifax Town, Blackburn Rovers, Derby County, Portsmouth, Stockport County (1927-1939).* 'Big hearted Arthur' joined from Derby in 1936 and played as a striker for two seasons until he lost his place to Jimmy McAlinden. Died in Derby in 1979 on his 72d birthday.

GUATELLI, Andrea

0 apps (2004-2005)
Career: *Fiorenzuola, Portsmouth, Oxford United (loan), FC Zurich (2007-date).* Italian goalie Guatelli was drafted in to provide cover for Shakka Hislop in 2004 but left less than two years later without making a league appearance. He did play for Jim Smith at Oxford United on loan before joining his current club, FC Zurich of the Swiss Super League.

GUNTER, Phil

365 apps, 2 goals (1951-1964)
Career: *Portsmouth, Aldershot (1951-1965).* Played over 300 games as a defender for Pompey before becoming a teacher in a local school then emigrated to Australia where he now lives in retirement. Phil's brother Dave played for Southampton but also worked at Fratton Park for many years before losing his job as part of a cost cutting exercise. (Some things never change!)
An England B international.

GUTHRIE, Jimmy

84 apps, 1 goal (1937-1938)
Career: *Portsmouth, Crystal Palace (1937-1946).* Played 84 times for Pompey most famously captaining the team to a 4-1 victory over Wolverhampton Wanderers in the 1939 FA Cup Final. A car accident later in 1939 and the suspension of competitive football during the Second World War put an end to his playing career. Throughout his career he was active in the Players' Union and he became the Union's fifth Chairman in August 1946 holding the position until 1957. His book 'Soccer Rebel', published in 1976, documents his time at the Players' Union and includes commentary about the subsequent work of the renamed Professional Footballers' Association and the state of the English game. Scottish wing half . He became a leading sports writer with the Sunday People but died in hospital in London on September 10, 1981.

HAINES, Willie

164 apps, 119 goals (1922-1928)
Career: *Portsmouth, Southampton (1922-1932).* Nick-named 'Farmer's Boy', Haines had an incredible strike rate and was the club's top scorer as they won the Third Division South Championship in 1923-1924. In 1935, Haines became the landlord of the Vine Inn, Frome, Somerset which he ran until 1949. He later moved into the dry cleaning business. In 1960, he became the president of the Portsmouth Supporters Club but died on 5th November 1974 aged 74.

HALL, Paul
216 apps, 42 goals (1993-1998)
Career: *Torquay United, Portsmouth, Coventry City, Walsall, Bury (loan), Sheffield United, WBA (loan), Walsall, Rushden & Diamonds, Tranmere Rovers, Chesterfield, Walsall, Wrexham (loan), Newport County (1990-2008).* Hall began his career as an apprentice at Torquay United before a £70,000 transfer brought him to Pompey in March 1993. Hall was to spend five happy seasons at Fratton Park and after some impressive displays gained a call up to the Jamaican national football team. He moved on to Coventry City for £300,000 in 1998. Became a football instructor at Solihull College when retired and in July 2010 he joined Conference side Mansfield Town as their Head Of Youth.

HAND, Eoin
307 apps, 14 goals (1968-1979)
Career: *Swindon Town, Portsmouth (1964-1978).* The former Eire player and manager, came across the water in October 1968 when his club, Drumcondra accepted Pompey's offer of £8,000. For the next seven years he was virtually a permanent fixture in the side and his consistent displays earned him a call up to the Eire side, for whom he made 19 appearances and was to later take over as National Team Manager. In 1976 he decided to move over to South Africa but returned to the club as player coach in December 1977. A career in management beckoned and he had stints in charge of Huddersfield Town, Shelbourne, Limerick and coached in South Africa. During his time with Limerick he was the 1980 Soccer Writers' Association of Ireland Personality of the Year and won the FAI Cup in 1982. Five years later, he was diagnosed with pancreatitis which has prompted him to gave up smoking and drinking. Having sold his house in Cowplain, he built a new home for himself in County Kerry and now works as an advisor for the Irish Football Association and commentates. for local radio and TV.

HARDYMAN, Paul
131 apps, 4 goals (1983-1989)
Career: *Portsmouth, Sunderland, Bristol Rovers, Wycombe Wanderers, Barnet. (1983-1997).* A local lad and fan who turned down Aston Villa to sign for Pompey. He preferred to complete his carpentry apprenticeship and earn his place at Fratton Park. When given his chance in March 1984, he made the first of many impressive displays which earned him a call up to the England Under 21 side and ultimately a £130,000 move to Sunderland. Hardyman also helped the club clinch promotion to the top flight in 1987. Bristol Rovers broke their transfer record to bring him back south but he ended his career at Barnet in 1996. He has since managed Slough Town, worked back at Fratton Park as part of the Football in the Community Team and then in the Centre of Excellence before being made redundant in 2009.

HARLAND, Stan
Coach (1978-1982)
Career: *Everton, Bradford City, Carlisle United, Swindon Town, Birmingham City, Yeovil Town (1959-1979).* Harland captained the Swindon Town side that beat Arsenal in 1969 to win the League Cup and worked on the coaching staff at Fratton Park under his former Swindon team-mate Frank Burrows. After leaving football he worked in the Supermarket business until his death from a heart attack on 30 August 2001 in Tintinhull, Somerset.

HARPER, Kevin

129 apps, 9 goals (1999-2005)
Career: *Hibernian, Derby County, Walsall, Portsmouth, Norwich City , Leicester City, Stoke City, Carlisle United, Walsall, Dunfermline Athletic (1992-2009).* A Scottish under 21 cap who showed glimpses of potential at Derby County which persuaded Pompey to part with £300,000 for his services. Injuries and sending-offs hampered his first season at Fratton Park but he became an integral part of the side that won the First Division title in 2002/3. He also earned two full caps with Scotland before being loaned out to Norwich City, Leicester City and then sold to Stoke City in 2005. He ended his playing career in 2009 when he was released by First Division side Dunfermline.

HARRIS, Harry

428 apps, 49 goals (1958-1970)
Career: *Newport County, Portsmouth, Newport County. (1954-1970).* Inside forward who clocked up over 500 league appearances for Pompey and Newport County in his sixteen year career. Freddie Cox made Harris one of his five new signings before the start of the 1958/9 season. He gave loyal service over the next decade including a period as club captain. Left the club to re-join Newport County in 1968 after almost 400 games, only to return for one more game in 1971. After his retirement in 1971 Harry ran a double glazing business in Leeds but sadly died in Magor in June 2004 aged 70.

HARRIS, Peter

518 apps, 208 goals (1947-1959)
Career: *Portsmouth (1946-1959).* Having watched Pompey as a child, it was right and fitting that he became one of the club's finest servants. An old fashioned winger who could fly past defenders, he also had a good eye for goal and bagged over 200 in his career. He played his part in both Championship years and he would have earned more than his brace of England caps if he had not been playing at the same time as Stanley Matthews and Tom Finney. A fantastic career was brought to an end in 1960 when he contracted TB and was forced to retire. Harris later lived in Hayling Island where he managed a restaurant complex, worked for a boat builders and then at a local day centre. Died on 2nd January 2003, aged 77.

HART, Paul

(Manager between February and November 2009.) After a career as an uncompromising defender, Hart moved into management and had already gained experience with Chesterfield, Nottingham Forest, Barnsley and Rushden before arriving at Fratton Park in March 2007. He was director of youth operations but took over as caretaker manager after Tony Adams' departure in February 2009. He was given a two year deal in the September but after a shocking run, he was sacked in November 2009. Less than two months later he was back in business as manager of QPR, albeit only for a matter of weeks. His next challenge was to help Crystal Palace avoid relegation after their boss, Neil Warnock, had ironically taken over the post vacated by Hart at QPR. Having achieved this feat with a draw on the last day of the season, he left the club.

HARTMANN, Matthew

0 (2006-2007)
Career: *Portsmouth, Weymouth (loan), Nottingham Forest, Bognor Regis Town (2006-2008).* An English-Filipino left back and has played for the Philippines at international level. He was a youth player at Pompey but was released without making a first team appearance. Signed for Bognor Regis upon his release.

PETER HARRIS

HATELEY, Mark

44 apps, 25 goals (1983-1984)
Career: *Coventry City, Portsmouth, Rangers, Queens Park Rangers, Leeds United, Rangers, Hull City (1978-1998).* Son of former Coventry City player Tony Hateley, Mark signed from the same East Midlands club for £200,000 in May 1983. He had already won England Under 21 caps and proved himself as a handful in the box and it didn't take long before he was tempted away from Fratton Park by the glamour of Spanish football. After an impressive 1983/4 season with Pompey which earned him the Player of the Year trophy, and a successful integration into the national side, AC Milan (managed by Fabio Capello) were prepared to part with £915,000 in June 1984. He later played for Monaco in France (managed by Arsene Wenger) before ending his career in Scotland with Rangers and then a few games for Ross County. Apart from a brief period as player manager with Hull he has been working in the media. His son Tom is now playing for Motherwell.
Player of the season in 1984.

HAYDOCK, Frank

79 apps, 1 goal (1965-1968)
Career: *Manchester United, Charlton Athletic, Portsmouth, Southend United (1959-1970).*
Strong centre half who had started with home town club Manchester United.

He arrived at Fratton Park via Charlton Athletic in December 1965 and put in steady displays over the next three years. later played for Southend before moving back to Lancashire to play for Fleetwood who also had Ray Pointer on their books. He settled in Blackpool and worked as a sales representative and then bought a taxi before retiring.

HAYWARD, Basil

51 apps, 4 goals (1958-1960)
Career: *Port Vale, Portsmouth, Yeovil Town (1946-1964).* Originally from the 'Potteries' Basil played 349 league games for local league side Port Vale before spending two years with Pompey. Became player-manager at Yeovil Town, managed non-league Bedford, Gillingham, and Telford United before becoming chief scout at Norwich City and then scout at Gillingham. He also played county cricket for Staffordshire as a left-arm medium pace bowler. Died on 9th December 1989 aged 61.

HAZARD, Micky

8 apps, 1 goal (1989-1990)
Career: *Tottenham Hotspur, Chelsea, Portsmouth, Swindon Town, Tottenham Hotspur (1978-1995).* Hazard was a stylish midfielder who had played for both Spurs and Chelsea when Chairman paid £100,000 to bring him to Hampshire. Scoring on his debut and then following this up with a brilliant display in his second game, he looked like a bargain buy. However, a fall out with new manager Frank Burrows resulted in his departure just a few games later. Has since worked as a youth coach for Spurs and Crystal Palace but is now working as a black cab driver in central London.

HEBBERD, Trevor

4 apps (1991-1992)
Career: *Southampton, Bolton Wanderers, Leicester City, Oxford United, Derby County, Portsmouth, Chesterfield, Lincoln City (1976-1994).* Well travellled midfielder who added Pompey to his list of clubs in 1991 but only made four appearances before ending his career at Chesterfield and finally Lincoln City. Upon retirement in 1995, Trevor took a job in a Leicester warehouse.

HEIKKINEN, Markus

2 apps (2002-2003)
Career: *Portsmouth (loan), Aberdeen, Luton Town, Rapid Vienna (1996-date).* Finnish international (although born in Sweden) centre back currently plays for SK Rapid Wien in the Austrian Bundesliga.

HEMMERMAN, Jeff

140 apps, 45 goals (1978-1982)
Career: *Hull City, Scunthorpe United (loan), Port Vale, Portsmouth, Cardiff City (1973-1983).* The corkscrew haired striker only ended up at Pompey due to administrative problems with the American indoor league, where he was due to play. The club needed to bring in replacements after relegation to the Third Division in 1978 and Hemmerman was seen as ideal cover for the existing strike-force. It wasn't long before he had edged himself into the frame and was being picked as first choice. In his four seasons, he notched up a creditable 45 goals in 140 appearances and it was a surprise when he was allowed to sign for Cardiff City in 1982. A knee ligament injury forced an early end to his footballing days and led to a career in physiotherapy. He then worked in Cardiff prior to setting up his own clinic in Newport, Gwent.

HENDERSON, Jackie

236 apps, 73 goals (1951-1958)
Career: *Portsmouth, Wolverhampton Wanderers, Arsenal, Fulham (1951-1963).* Initially a centre forward, he also played as an inside forward and left-winger. With lightening pace he was a constant threat as well as being a capable goalscorer. This combination cemented his position in the team but also earned him seven full Scottish caps . Moves to Wolves and Arsenal followed but a broken leg while playing for Fulham ended his career in 1963. Moved to Dorset and turned out for Dorchester Town while working as a storeman for a local builders merchants in Poole. He lived in Broadstone until his death in January 2005.

HENDON, Ian

4 apps (1991-1992)
Career: *Tottenham H Portsmouth, Leyton Orient, Barnsley, Leyton O, Birmingham C, Notts County, Northampton Town, Barnet, Peterborough United, Barnet (1989-2009).* A former England Under 21 international who played four games for Pompey during a loan from Tottenham Hotspur. Managed Barnet and Dover and is now assistant manager at Gillingham.

Photo: Ben Sutherland

HENWOOD, Rodney
2 apps (1953-1954)
Career: *Kingston Boys Club, Portsmouth, Salisbury (1950-1953).* Portsmouth born left back worked as a carpenter while playing semi-professionally for Pompey. Stayed in the same trade until his retirement. Also turned out for the Pompey ex-pros until he was 50.

HIGHAM, Peter
1 app (1949-1950)
Career: *Wigan Athletic, Portsmouth, Bolton Wanderers, Preston North End, Nottingham Forest, Doncaster Rovers (1949-1958).* Was with Pompey for four months while serving with the Royal Marines in Eastney. Although he only made one appearance he went on to enjoy almost a decade of League football with four clubs. During this time he gained his full FA coaching badge and shared his knowledge with American school kids every summer. Went on to become a teacher of Mathematics and PE and then to work with the physically handicapped. Now lives in retirement on Southport seafront.

HILAIRE, Vince
168 apps, 26 goals (1984-1988)
Career: *Crystal Palace, Luton Town, Portsmouth, Leeds United, Stoke City, Exeter City (1976-1993).* One of the first black players to establish himself in the League. Former England Under 21 international Hilaire was given his chance as a 17 year old by Crystal Palace and was a member of their 'Team of the Eighties'. Popular with the fans because of his lightening pace and tight ball control, he was named the London club's Player of the Year in 1979 and 1980. He moved to Pompey for £100,000 in November 1984 after playing a handful of games for Luton Town. Was then an integral part of the promotion winning side in 1987. The following year he was transferred to Leeds United in a £190,000 deal but his career then wound down at Stoke City with former boss Alan Ball and finally, in the west country with Exeter City. Became player and joint manager of Waterlooville with former Palace and Pompey team-mate Billy Gilbert. Has worked for a cable television company in Portsmouth and helped with match-day hospitality at Fratton Park. His daughter Danielle was a Soccerette on Soccer AM.

HILEY, Scott
80 apps (1999-2002)
Career: *Exeter City, Birmingham City, Manchester City, Southampton, Portsmouth, Exeter City (1986-2008).* Started his League career with Exeter City and it was not until he was 24 years old that he ventured out of his native Devon - to follow his manager Terry Cooper to Birmingham City. An injury riddled couple of years with Manchester City followed before he joined Pompey on for a nominal fee in December 1999. Having been made captain, he was a bright spot in a side that was struggling and was the club's Player of the Year in his first season. He eventually returned to see out the remaining days of his career at Exeter City and still plays for their Legend's team today. Scott now runs a Bed & Breakfast with his wife Tina in the village of Clyst St Mary just outside Exeter. *Player of the season in 2001.*

HILLIER, David
74 apps, 7 goals (1996-1999)
Career: *Arsenal, Portsmouth, Bristol Rovers, Barnet. (1988-2003).* Having played 142 matches for Arsenal, Hillier was sold to Pompey for £250,000. He played 61 matches in two and a half years . He had a spell at Bristol Rovers and Barnet before retiring in 2003. He now works as a fireman in the Bristol area and manages non-league team, Oldland Abbotonians. *England under 21 international.*

HINDMARCH, Billy
61 apps (1946-1951)
Career: *Portsmouth, Swindon Town (1946-1951).* A reliable full back who signed forms in 1939 but had to wait until after the war to make his debut (in 1946). Played 55 games in total over the next four years before joining Swindon in 1951. Later returned to his native north-east to take on the 'Vulcan' public house in Spennymoor. Died in 1994

HINDMARCH, Rob
2 apps (1983-1984)
Career: *Sunderland, Portsmouth, Derby County, Wolverhampton Wanderers (1977-1994).* Made two appearances on loan from Sunderland in the 1980's but blossomed as a hard-working and reliable defender later in his career with Derby and Wolves. Worked for Wolves in their Centre of Excellence. He then moved to the States to coach youngsters in New Jersey where he died after a long battle against motor neurone disease in November 2002 aged only 41.

HINSHELWOOD, Danny

5 apps (1995-1996)
Career: *Nottingham Forest, Portsmouth, Torquay United, Brighton (1992-1999).* A member of the famous footballing Hinshelwood family, Danny was once an apprentice at Nottingham Forest where one of his duties was to walk Brian Clough's dog. He became manager of Selsey in 2004 and also took on the role of assistant manager of the Sussex county side.

HIRON, Ray

364 apps, 117 goals (1964-1975)
Career: *Portsmouth, Reading (1964-1977).* A prolific goalscorer and local lad who was 6ft 2in tall but only weighed 11 stone. Having signed terms in his lunch hour while working at the dockyard, he went on to become one of the club's most consistent performers through the late 60's and early 70's. His gangly frame and long legs caused problems for opposing defenders and earned him over 100 league goals including four in one game against Norwich City in 1968/9. When John Deacon brought in a flurry of new faces, it was time for the old guard to be released. Fittingly, Ray scored both the goals that defeated south coast rivals Southampton in his testimonial match at the end of the 1974/5 season. Played the last three years of his career at Reading and later spent 25 years working as a manager at the Mountbatten Sports Centre.

HISLOP, Shaka

100 apps (2002-2004)
Career: *Reading, Newcastle United, West Ham United, Portsmouth, West Ham United. (1992-2006).* Kept goal for the First Division title winning side in 2002/3 having arrived from Newcastle United the previous year. Retained the number 1 jersey until Alain Perrin took over as boss and preferred Sander Westerveld. An international with Trinidad & Tobago, Hislop then returned to his old club West Ham. He is now working in the media for ESPN and regularly commentates on Italian and Spanish League matches. Was named the as the first winner of the PFA Special Merit Award in 2005 for his services to football and has been inducted into Trinidad & Tobago's Hall of Fame.
England Under 21 & full international with Trinidad & Tobago.

HOGG, Graeme

110 apps, 2 goals (1988-1991)
Career: *Manchester United, WBA (loan), Portsmouth, Heart of Midlothian, Notts County, Brentford (1984-1998).* Former Scotland Under-21 international whose 6ft 1in frame slotted comfortably into the back four, following a £150,000 move from Manchester United. He made over 100 appearances under three different managers but was released when the fourth, Jim Smith, accepted a £200,000 bid from Hearts. Is still living in Scotland and works as a television engineer.

HORN, Graham

26 apps (1972-1973)
Career: *Arsenal, Portsmouth, Luton Town, Brentford, Los Angeles Aztecs, Charlton Athletic, Kettering Town, Southend United, Aldershot, Torquay United (1972-1983).* Was only 17 when Arsenal allowed him to join Pompey on loan for the season. Even then, he was 6ft 2in tall and weighed 14 stones. Despite a series of impressive performances, it came as a shock when he decided to join Luton Town on a permanent deal after only 22 games. He ended his league career at Torquay United and has been a residential social worker for Devon County Council since 1994.

HORNE, Barry

79 apps, 7 goals (1987-1989)
Career: *Wrexham, Portsmouth, Southampton, Everton, Birmingham City, Huddersfield Town, Sheffield Wednesday, Kidderminster Harriers, Walsall (1984-2001).* Pompey provided the launchpad for the Welshman's career. During his stay he successfully made the transition from the Fourth Division to the rigours of First Division football. He also won the first of his 59 Welsh caps and won the player of the season award in 1987/8. Before turning pro Horne had obtained a first-class university degree in chemistry from the University of Liverpool and he now puts that to good use as a Physics and Chemistry teacher at the King's School, Chester. He can also be heard on Merseyside radio station Radio City 96.7 and writes a football column in the Liverpool Echo newspaper. At one time he was chairman of the Professional Footballers Association.
Player of the season in 1988.

Ray Hiron

Photo: stubramley

HOUGH, Ted

1 app (1931-1932)
Career: *Southampton, Portsmouth, Bristol Rovers. (1921-1933).* Signed from Southampton for the princely sum of £200 in 1931 but only made one appearance before moving on to Bristol Rovers. Ted did return to the area and worked as a fitter's mate in a local power station. Died on 3rd September 1978 aged 78.

HOULT, Russell

45 apps (1999-2001)
Career: *Leicester City, Derby County, Portsmouth, West Bromwich Albion, Stoke City, Notts County, Darlington (loan), plus many other loan spells to various clubs (1991- date).* Hoult has kept goal for eleven league clubs including a spell with Pompey at the turn of the century. His personal life has taken up many column inches in the tabloids over the years. There have been a number of revelations including an accusation that he took place in an orgy dressed in his West Brom shirt! He was released by Notts County in May 2010.

HOWE, Eddie

2 apps (2001-2003)
Career: *Bournemouth, Portsmouth, Bournemouth (1994-2007).* Before becoming the youngest manager in the league with AFC Bournemouth, Howe had been a player with the club for most of his professional career. The only break was an injury spoilt spell at Fratton Park. He had become Harry Redknapp's first signing in 2002 but the former England Under 21 international incurred damage to one of his knees in an early game and never managed to establish himself back in the side. In 2004 after an appeal from their Chairman, Bournemouth fans pledged a total of £13,500 to pay for his transfer back to Dean Court. Two years later, at the age of 29, he was promoted to player-coach by Kevin Bond but lost his job when Bond was sacked in September 2008. New boss Jimmy Quinn asked him to return to look after the Youth Team but his staff member became his replacement in January 2009.

HOWE, Ernie

41 apps, 5 goals (1982-1984)
Career: *Fulham, Queens Park Rangers, Portsmouth (1973-1984).* London born defender who started his career in illustrious company - he was on Fulham's books at the same time as George Best and Rodney Marsh. He also featured in the 1975 FA Cup final before moving to QPR and then Pompey. Having scored on his debut, he helped win the Third Division championship in 1982/3. Spent 13 years at Basingstoke Town and then a much shorter spell at Sutton United until March 2008. Later set up a building business with his brother in law. His son Aaron plays in goal for for Havant & Waterlooville.

HOWELLS, Ron

71 apps, 2 goals (1958-1961)
Career: *Wolverhampton Wanderers, Portsmouth, Scunthorpe United, Walsall (1955-1963).* Welshman who played in the Pompey team that was relegated from the first division in 1960. It was later in his career that he hit the headlines for all the wrong reasons. While registered as a Walsall player, Howells became embroiled in a betting scandal and was suspended for life by the Football League.

HUMPSTON, Ron

9 apps (1947-1951)
Career: *Portsmouth, Huddersfield Town (1947-1951).* Former naval physical training instructor who was signed as cover for regular goalkeeper Ernie Butler in 1946. Was at the club during the Championship years but was only called upon a handful of times before moving to Northampton Town. Later managed Gravesend,Gloucester City, Oxford City and then became a sports ground manager while coaching part time. Retired to live the quiet life in Chipping Campden, Gloucestershire.

Hunter, George

8 apps 0 goals
Career: *Aston Villa. Oldham Athletic. Chelsea, Manchester United, Portsmouth. (1908-1922).* A fiery wing half nicknamed 'Cocky' who had suffered from discipline problems before his time at Pompey, and it is reported that his manager nor his team mates could control him. Wrote a light hearted football book before going onto serve as a sergeant-major in the army during the World War One seeing action in France and Gallipoli. The Indian born enigma served three months hard labour in August 1930 for deserting his wife and children and died in February 1934 aged 46.

HUNT, Ralph

5 apps (1952-1954)
Career: *Portsmouth, Bournemouth, Norwich City, Derby County, Grimsby Town, Swindon Town, Port Vale, Newport County, Chesterfield (1952-1964).* Centre forward whose goal-scoring career took off after he left Fratton Park. He only managed five starts in his two years as a professional before moving along the coast to play for Bournemouth. It was while with his next club, Norwich City that he started to regularly hit the back of the net - he scored 67 goals in 124 league matches, and his 31 goals in the 1955-56 season is still a club record. Portsmouth boy Hunt, then took his goal scoring boots around the country, eventually signing for Chesterfield in 1964. He was tragically killed in a car accident in the same year, he was only 31 at the time.

HUNTER, John

37 apps, 11 goals (1905-1907)
Career: *Liverpool, Heart of Midlothian, Woolwich Arsenal, Portsmouth, Dundee, Clyde (1896-1911).* John 'Sailor' Hunter is still a legend in Motherwell. He was the club's first and longest-serving manager, guiding them to their only League title in the 1931-32 season. Sailor remained at Fir Park as club secretary until his retirement in 1959 at the age of 80. The club granted him a weekly pension upon his retirement. He died in January 1966 aged 87.

IGOE, Sammy

177 apps, 11 goals (1994-2000)
Career: *Portsmouth, Reading, Luton Town (loan), Swindon Town, Millwall, Bristol Rovers, Hereford United (loan), Bournemouth (1994-date).* Pompey was Sammy's first club but Jim Smith feared that at 5ft 6in, he was too short to make an impact as a professional. Despite this assessment, he went on to enjoy a career that spanned over ten years and took in eight League clubs. He was Steve Claridge's only signing during his 23 days in charge at Millwall and ended his playing days at Bournemouth. Then signed for Havant & Waterlooville, in June 2010.

ILIC, Sasa

7 apps (2001-2002)
Career: *Charlton Athletic, West Ham United, Portsmouth, Barnsley, Blackpool. Aberdeen, Leeds United (1997-2005).* A goalkeeper who rolled up at Charlton asking for a trial and ended up saving a penalty which got them promoted to the Premier League. He is now an entrepreneur with interests that include an interior design company and in the banking world as a consultant with Austrian-based Hypo Group Alpe-Adria. ilic has also acted in a couple of low budget films.

JACKSON, Bob

(Manager between 1947 and 1952)
Was manager of the Championship winning sides of 1948/9 and 1949/50. Moved to Hull City in a similar role in 1952 but despite their ambition, his three years at the club could not replicate the success that he had achieved with Pompey.

JAMES, David

Made some world class saves during his Fratton Park stay and it was a real shame that circumstances prompted his departure. Now with Bristol City.

Nicky Jennings

JAMES, Keith

6 apps (1978-1980)
Career: *Portsmouth, Norwich City (1978-1979).* Despite early promise, Keith only managed six appearances as a professional. He had previously played in the same England Youth team as Alan Knight and Paul Walsh. The Hillingdon born former right back is now believed to living in Pinner, Middlesex.

JENNINGS, Nicky

227 apps, 49 goals (1966-1973)
Career: *Plymouth Argyle, Portsmouth, Aldershot, Exeter City (1963-1977).* Tricky winger who hailed from the west country and made the outside left position his own during his seven years with the club. He won the Player of the Season award in 1970 and was popular with the fans. His reign came to an end when Peter Marinello was signed from Arsenal and he eventually returned to the south west to end his career at Exeter City. Then studied Social Policy at University and spent many years in Wimborne Minster, working as a Probation Officer and Family Court advisor. *Player of the season in 1970.*

Photo: choonming

JOHNSON, Glen

100 apps, 4 goals (2006-2009)
Career: *West Ham United, Millwall (loan), Chelsea, Portsmouth, Liverpool (2001-date).* With is career stagnating at Chelsea he became one of the classiest defenders to pull on a Pompey shirt. With finances being squeezed, it was disappointing but no real surprise when he signed for Liverpool for a reported £18 million in June 2009.
Player of the season in 2009.

David James and Ray Crawford

KABOUL, Younes

39 apps, 4 goals (2008-2010)
Career: *Auxerre, Tottenham Hotspur, Portsmouth, Tottenham Hotspur (2004-date).* Another player who made the move from Spurs in 2008. The former French Under 21 international signed for £6 million in August of that year but returned to White Hart Lane for £3.5 million more than the original purchase price less than two years later.

KAMARA, Chris

811 apps, 9 goals (1975-77 and 1981-2)
Career: *Portsmouth, Swindon Town, Portsmouth, Brentford, Swindon Town, Stoke City, Leeds United, Luton Town, Sheffield United, Bradford City (1975-1995).* Former dockyard apprentice who was spotted by Ray Crawford and the Middlesbrough born striker flourished in his youth set up. He played for nine clubs in a 20 year career and had two spells at Fratton Park. Later managed both Bradford City and Stoke City, but is now working as a presenter and commentator for Sky. Changed his surname to Cabagna in response to an internet campaign before the 2010 World Cup finals in the hope that it would improve England's chances!

Chris Kamara

KAMARA, Diomansy

29 apps , 6 goals (2004-2005)
Career: *Red Star 93, Catanzaro, Modena, Portsmouth, WBA, Fulham, Celtic (loan) (1998-date).* Became the club's record signing when a fee of £2.5 million was paid to Italian side Modena. The French-Senegalese striker struggled to find consistent form and was troubled by a series of injuries and after less than a year was sold on to West Brom. Currently registered as a Fulham player but joined Celtic on loan in February 2010.

Old footballers in a pub - surely not?

KARADAS, Azar

20 apps, 1 goal (2005-2006)
Career: *Brann, Rosenborg, Benfica,
Portsmouth (loan), Kaiserslautern (loan),
Brann, Kasimpasa (1999-date).* Norwegian
player of Turkish origin spent a season on
loan from Portuguese giants Benfica. In his
short stay he did manage to score one
spectacular goal against Bolton Wanderers to
earn a much needed point. Karadas later
played in Norway and won the national title
with Brann. In 2009 he penned a three year
deal to play for his current club Kasýmpaþa
S.K. in Turkey.

KAWAGUCHI, Yoshikatsu

13 apps (2001-2002)
Career: *Yokohama F. Marinos, Portsmouth,
FC Nordsjælland, Júbilo Iwata. (1994-date).*
Yoshi arrived at Fratton Park in a blaze of
publicity and with the hope that he would
stop the goals but also provide additional
commercial revenue from shirt sales in the Far
East. Despite his best efforts, neither was
achieved during his short stay. Already an
established Japanese international keeper, no
one could fault his attitude - he tried his
hardest and always with a smile on his face.
Unfortunately, this could not make up for the
fact that the goals were being leaked at an
alarming rate and it was not long before he
was replaced by Dave Beasant. Moved on to
play in Denmark, but the crowd showed his
their appreciation by giving him a standing
ovation in his last match, having appeared as
a second half substitute in the final game of
the 2002/3 season (during which time,
ironically, he kept a clean sheet). Still playing
in Japan, he was one of several ex-Pompey
players to appear in the 2010 World Cup.

KEENE, James

2 apps (2004-2005)
Career: *Portsmouth, Kidderminster (loan),
Boston United (loan), GAIS (loan), Elfsborg
(2004-date).* Former Pompey youngster who
has made a name for himself in Sweden. He is
better known in this country for miskicking a
ball which then hit Harry Redknapp during a
television interview. After bawling at the
player Harry turned to the camera and
quoted the memorable phrase "No wonder
he's still in the ****** reserves".

Since the incident, there has been some
dispute as to which player was the true
culprit. The Somerset born striker was then
sent out on loan to Swedish side GAIS and
ended the season as their top scorer. This
resulted in permanent move to Scandanavia
and a five year deal to play for IF Elfsborg.

KELLARD, Bobby

176 apps, 18 goals (1966-1975)
Career: *Southend United, Crystal Palace,
Ipswich Town, Portsmouth, Bristol City,
Leicester City, Crystal Palace, Portsmouth,
Hereford United, Torquay United (1959-
1975).* In a nine club career than spanned
fifteen years, Kellard played over 500 games
and had two spells at Pompey. Originally
signed as a winger, but it was as a battling
midfielder that he will be remembered. His
days in the league came to a close in 1975
and was signed by Jimmy Greaves to play for
Chelmsford City. later ran a taxi business in
Southend and then bought and sold antiques
before moving to Spain.

KELLER, Marc

3 apps (2000-2001)
Career: *Mulhouse, Strasbourg, Karlsrhure,
West Ham, Portsmouth, Blackburn Rovers
(1987-2002).* French midfielder who played
three games on loan from West Ham in Tony
pulis' reign. He won six caps for his country
and played in France, Germany and England
before retiring from the game. Keller later
became Director-General of RC Strasbourg
and AS Monaco

KELLY, Mark

57 apps, 2 goals (1987-1991)
Career: *Portsmouth, Sligo Rovers,
Farnborough Town, Finn Harps (1987-2001).*
Alan Ball once described the Republic of
Ireland winger as "the next George Best"
which probably raised both expectation and
pressure on the 18 year old. Despite rumours
of interest from Arsenal, he struggled to make
a regular impact. His situation was not helped
by a series of niggling injuries and it was
damage to a knee that prematurely ended his
career in 1991. Later he played part time for
Sligo Rovers and Farnborough Town F.C. and
worked as head of youth development at
Fratton Park.

PORTSMOUTH.

A. E. KNIGHT.

KEMP, David

74 apps, 38 goals (1976-1978)
Career: *Crystal Palace, Portsmouth, Carlisle United, Plymouth Argyle, Gillingham, Brentford (1974-1981).* Became a goalscoring hero following his arrival from Crystal Palace in a deal that took George Graham to Selhurst Park. A former Chelsea youngster, Kemp was top scorer in both 1976/7 and 1977/8 and it was a sad day when he moved to Carlisle United in March 1978. Salt was rubbed in the wounds when he returned to Fratton Park shortly afterwards and scored for his new club in a 3-3 draw. Frank Burrows did try to sign him during his tenure but it was not until he had retired from playing that the popular striker's name was again added to the payroll, this time as a member of the coaching staff. Has since managed Norwegian side Norrköping, Plymouth Argyle and Oxford United but has been Assistant Manager to his former Pompey boss, Tony Pulis, at Stoke City since July 2010.

KENNEDY, Bill

1 app (1932-1933)
Career: *Portsmouth, Carlisle United, Crewe Alexandra, Southampton (1932-1938).* He played one game for Pompey before moving north to Carlisle United in 1933. After a period with Hamilton Academical, he returned to the Southampton area and joined the merchant navy, serving on RMS Queen Mary. In 1962 he left the service and settled in Southampton working at Mullard in Millbrook. He died in Southampton on 12th December 1989, aged 77.

KENNEDY, Mick

144 apps, 5 goals (1984-1988)
Career: *Halifax Town, Huddersfield Town, Middlesbrough, Portsmouth, Bradford City, Leicester City, Luton Town, Stoke City, Chesterfield, Wigan Athletic (1978-1994).* Kennedy took few prisoners as a no-nonsense hard tackling midfielder. This earned him the wrath of many a referee but also the seal of approval from the club's supporters. As a Republic of Ireland international, he won two caps and could also take a mean penalty. Now lives in County Clare in Ireland and coaches a local team, Lifford A.F.C. having previously run his own soccer school in the area.

KERR, John

6 apps (1987-1988)
Career: *Portsmouth, Peterborough United (loan), Wycombe Wanderers, Linfield, Boulogne-Sur-Mer, Hamilton Steelers, San Diego Sockers (indoor), Millwall, Walsall, Dallas Burn, New England Revolution, Boston Bulldogs (1987-1999).* The first American player to play in the First Division, Kerr only managed a handful of games before being released. He is now head coach of the Duke University soccer team.

Photo: Rockface

KIELY, Dean

17 apps (2005-2007)
Career: *Coventry City, Ipswich Town (loan), York City, Bury, Charlton Athletic, Portsmouth, Luton Town (loan), West Bromwich Albion (1987-date).* Kiely had played over 500 League games before coming to Pompey's rescue in 2006. He played a major role in helping the struggling team avoid relegation. However, when David James arrived at the club, Kiely opted to move elsewhere in a bid to secure first team football. He now plays for West Bromwich Albion. His son Chris is also a keeper and plays for Halesowen Town
English-born Kiely was called up to the England under-17 squad in 1986, but later went on to represent the Republic of Ireland at full international level

KNIGHT, Alan

799 apps (1979-2000)
Career: *Portsmouth (1978-2000).* 'The
Legend' will go down in Pompey history as
not only one of the best goalkeepers to have
played for the club but also one of it's most
loyal servants. Over 20 plus years he played
over 800 games and broke Peter Bonetti's
record for the number of appearances by a
goalkeeper for one club. After signing
professional terms on his sixteenth birthday,
the great shot-stopper had to wait patiently as
Peter Mellor's understudy before being given
a decent run in the first team. When his
chance finally came in the early eighties he
shone and never let the jersey go again until
his retirement in 1980. As well as winning a
place in the hearts of Pompey fans of all ages,
Knightsie also gained two Under 21 caps with
England, an honourary degree from
Portsmouth University, and an MBE for his
services to football in the 2001 New Years
Honours List. He stayed on at Fratton Park as
goalkeeping coach and has since helped
keepers in America, Havant, Dorchester,
Bournemouth. In December 2009, he agreed
to join fellow Pompey old boy Kevin Dillon at
League Two side Aldershot Town and is now
their goalkeeping coach .
Player of the season in 1982, 1995, and 1996.

KOROMAN, Ognjen

4 apps, 1 goal (2006-2007)
Career: *Radnički Kragujevac, Spartak
Subotica, OFK Beograd, Dynamo Moscow,
Krylia Sovetov Samara, Terek Grozny,
Portsmouth (loan), Red Star Belgrade,
Incheon United (1997-date).* Serbian
international whose performances at the 2006
World Cup were overshadowed by waving
imaginary yellow cards in the hope of
persuading the referee to book opposing
players. He was registered as a Pompey
player at the time thanks to a loan
arrangement with Russian club FC Terek
Grozny. Scored a cracking goal against
Liverpool but never quite established himself
and joined Red Star Belgrade the following
year. Now plays for Incheon United in Korea.

KRANJCAR, Niko

99 apps, 12 goals (2006-2009)
Career: *Dynamo Zagreb, Hajduk Split,
Portsmouth, Tottenham Hotspur. (2001-date).*
A £3.5 purchase from Hajduk Split in 2006,
Nico was undoubtedly a world class player on
his day. Always capable of creating an opening
from nothing, the Croatian international was a
key player in the 2008 FA Cup win and it was
no surprise when 'larger' clubs started to
show interest. A move became more likely
when he publicly stated his intention to leave
when his contract expired. Tottenham Hotspur
took advantage of the situation in September
2009 and picked him up for a modest £2.5 - a
fraction of his true worth.

KRISTENSEN, Bjorn

90 apps, 5 goals (1992-1995)
Career: *AGF Aarhus, Newcastle United,
Bristol City, Portsmouth, Aalborg BK, Aarhus
Fremad (1982-1997).* "Benny" followed
former Newcastle United boss Jim Smith to
Fratton Park and stayed a couple of seasons
during which time he played in midfield and
defence. A Danish international, Kristensen
played for his country in the 1988 European
Championship and won a total of 20 caps. He
returned to Denmark where he helped
Aarhus Fremad win promotion to the Danish
top division. Worked as a sales manager for
Hummel International for four years and is
now owner of The Ranch and a director of
Radio100FM Østjylland.

KUHL, Martin

184 apps, 29 goals (1988-1993)
Career: *Birmingham City, Sheffield United, Watford, Portsmouth, Derby County, Notts County, Bristol City (1983-1987).* A popular midfielder who was voted Player of the season in 1991. It is a shame that his missed penalty kick in the 1992 FA Cup semi-final clouded an otherwise successful five year stay. Was known as a 'hard man' in midfield and certainly took no prisoners. It was this tag that persuaded him to accept an offer to play in Hong Kong in an attempt to shake off the reputation towards the end of his career. He never did return to play in the league and finished up in non-league soccer before qualifying for his coaching badges. Coached at Aldershot and then followed Gary Waddock to Wycombe Wanderers.
Player of the season in 1991.

KYZERIDIS, Nicos

2 apps, 2 goals (1998)
Career: *Naoussa, Panilakos, Portsmouth (1990's).* After an impressive debut, Greek forward Kyzeridis only lasted another four months before returning home. He has since played for a number of clubs and in 2005 was reported to be playing for Veria in the country's third level.

LAIDLAW, Joe

75 apps, 23 goals (1979-1981)
Career: *Middlesbrough, Carlisle, Doncaster, Portsmouth, Hereford, Mansfield (1967-1982).* Former midfield dynamo enjoyed a fifteen year career which included a three year stay at Pompey. He had also tasted First Division football with the most unlikely of sides, Carlisle United.

Frank Burrows paid Doncaster Rovers £15,000 in 1979 and promptly made his new acquisition club captain. He led the side to promotion from the Fourth Division and was voted Player of the Season in 1979-80. His 60 games at the club included standing in for Peter Mellor in one game and saw him also bag 19 goals before moving on to Hereford United. At the end of his playing days he returned south as manager for Petersfield, Chichester City and Selsea. Still lives in the area and works as a roofer.
Player of the season in 1980

LAMBOURDE, Bernard

6 apps (2000-2001)
Career: *Cannes, Angers, Cannes, Bordeaux, Chelsea, Portsmouth, Bastia, Nancy, Al Wahdu (1991-2003).* Played six games on loan from Chelsea, who had paid Bordeaux £1.6 million for his services. However, he was sold on to Bastia in his native France shortly after returning to Stamford Bridge. Ended his playing days in Saudi Arabia with Al-Whada FC. Retired in 2003 to became a member of the French Beach Football squad. Now lives in the South of France and has invested in a company that sells hardware for motor homes.

LANGE, Tony

Career: *Charlton Athletic, Aldershot, Wolverhampton Wanderers, Aldershot, Torquay United, Portsmouth, West Bromwich Albion, Fulham (1982-1997).* Goalkeeper who played over 250 league games in his career. Joined Pompey on loan in 1992 but did not make any first team appearances. Later worked as a landscape gardener and then became a revenue protection officer for Southern Railways.

LATHAN, John

62 apps, 4 goals (1978-1980)
Career: *Sunderland, Mansfield Town, Carlisle United, Barnsley, Portsmouth, Mansfield Town (1969-1979).* Bustling midfielder and one time captain who joined from Carlisle in 1978 as part of the deal that took David Kemp in the opposite direction. Ended his career at Mansfield Town. Lived in New York and coached at the Manhattan Soccer Club, before becoming a physio, opening his own business. Moved to Australia to live in Sydney.

LAUREN, Bissan

30 apps (2006-2009)
Career: *Mallorca, Arsenal, Portsmouth, Cordoba CF (1995-date).* Cameroonian right back who cost the club £500,000 in 2007 when he agreed to join from Arsenal. Played regularly in his first season but lost his place following the arrival of Glen Johnson and was released at the end of the 2008/9 season. Lauren signed for Spanish second division side Cordoba CF in March 2010.

LAWLER, Chris

40 apps (1975-1977)
Career: *Liverpool, Portsmouth, Stockport County (1960-1978).* With a full trophy cabinet gained from a hugely successful career with Liverpool, right-back Lawler was persuaded to make the move south to Fratton Park by old team-mate Ian St John. Sadly, he could not help prevent the club from sliding down two divisions and was released when Jimmy Dickinson took over following 'the Saint''s dismissal. His career ended more brightly at Stockport County and when he finally hung up his boots he returned to Anfield to join their coaching staff. In recent years, his vast experience has been helping to train young kids in Skelmersdale and to entertain audiences as part of the Bill Shankly Story, a stage show with Ian Callaghan, Ian St John and Ron Yeats.

LAWRENCE, George

14 apps (1992-1993)
Career: *Southampton, Oxford United, Southampton, Millwall, Bournemouth, Portsmouth, Hibernians (Malta) (1980-1996).* In 1993, he made 14 appearances for Portsmouth, all from the substitutes' bench (without scoring). He finished his playing career with a spell in Malta, playing with Hibernians F.C. where he won two consecutive titles, followed by lower-league football. Since retiring from playing professionally, he has continued to turn out in veterans' matches as well as earning a living as a player's agent.

LEATHER, Maurice

19 apps (1950-1953)
Former England Youth goalie who hailed from Southampton but was stationed at Hilsea during his National Service and agreed to join Pompey. Was one of the smallest keepers in the League and was mainly used as an understudy for Ernie Butler. Made his debut at Everton in September 1950 but only made less than 20 more appearances before dropping down to non-league football with Sandown on the Isle of Wight.

Hall of Fame winners and organisers.

Photo: Rowan Farnham-Long

LEE, David

5 apps (1994-1995)
Career: *Chelsea, Reading, Plymouth Argyle, Portsmouth, Sheffield United, Bristol Rovers, Crystal Palace, Exeter City (1988-2000).* Played four games on loan from Chelsea in 1994-5. David is now back in his native Bristol working as a full time development coach with Bristol City FC over-seeing the 18-21 year-olds.

LEVER, Eddie

(Manager between 1952 and 1958.)
Was manager for six years during which time he took the club to the fifth round of the FA Cup, was in charge of the first match ever to be held under floodlights, and was responsible for bringing Derek Dougan over from Ireland. However, possibly his greatest achievement was made while working as a schoolteacher before his management days. He spotted the potential of a young player called Jimmy Dickinson and suggested that the club should consider having a look at him.

LEWIS, Brian

210 apps, 32 goals (1963-67 and 1971-1975)
Career: *Crystal Palace, Portsmouth, Coventry City, Luton Town, Oxford United, Colchester United, Portsmouth (1960-1974).* A versatile player who enjoyed two separate spells at Fratton Park. The first, between 1963 and 1966 saw him become a regular first team member following his £8,000 transfer from Crystal Palace. He reluctantly moved to Coventry City in England's World Cup year when Pompey accepted an offer of £15,000 plus Ray Pointer from the Sky Blues. Was a member of the giant killing Fourth Division Colchester team that stunned First Division Leeds United (with goals scored by Portsmouth born Dave Simmonds and Ray Crawford). Worked as a salesman in a furniture showroom in Bournemouth until his death from cancer in 1988 aged 55. It was claimed that he was the player immortalised on the sign that hung above the Pompey Arms for many years. Although this has always been the subject of fierce debate, with others believing that it was in fact Albert McCann.

LEWORTHY, Dave

1 app 0 goals (1981)
Career: *Portsmouth, Tottenham Hotspur, Oxford United, Shrewsbury Town, Reading (1981-1993).* An England semi professional international and local lad who had been banging in the goals for the reserves but never managed to break into the first team. A drop down to local football with Fareham Town re-vitalised his career, earning a move to Tottenham Hotspur. He played for three more clubs professionally and was a massive hit with a number of non-league sides before signing for Havant & Waterlooville in 2000. Has since managed Banstead and Croydon.

LEY, George

204 apps, 11 goals (1966-1973)
Career: *Exeter City, Portsmouth, Brighton, Gillingham (1963-1975).* Left back who once topped a poll for best looking footballer, beating off the challenge of other players such as George Best! Originally from Exeter, Ley had joined Pompey from his local club in an £8,000 deal in 1967. Enjoyed five years at Fratton Park and was popular with the fans, although he was pipped to the club's first Player of the Year award by Ray Pointer. Later had a spell as Luton Town's youth coach before emigrating to the United States where he has coached various teams. He had played for a number of US clubs at the tail end of his career and is still there today, living in Austin, Texas and working as Director of Coaching for the Crossfire Soccer Club.

George Ley in action

LILL, Mickey

43 apps, 7 goals (1962-1965)

Career: *Wolverhampton Wanderers, Everton, Plymouth Argyle, Portsmouth (1954-1965).* Lill had been picked for the England youth team by George Smith and it was the same man that brought him to Fratton Park in 1963. He could play on either wing and stayed for three seasons. He then left English football to join Germiston Callies in South Africa. as a player and later to become their coach and a PE teacher just outside Johannesburg. He died after a battle against cancer in October 2004, aged 68.

LITTLE, Glen

8 apps (2008-2009)

Career: *Crystal Palace, Glentoran, Burnley, Reading, Portsmouth, Reading (loan), Sheffield United (1994-date).* A winger who had his best days at Burnley and Reading signed a one year deal in June 2008 but failed to edge his way into the first team and returned to Reading the following year. Signed for Aldershot in July 2010.

LOVELL, Steve

36 apps, 4 goals (1999-2002)

Career: *Bournemouth, Portsmouth, Exeter City (loan), Sheffield United (loan), QPR (loan), Dundee, Aberdeen, Falkirk, Partick Thistle. (1998-date).* A 6ft 1inch striker who was snapped up from Bournemouth after only one league appearance. Having paid out £250,000, manager Alan Ball only used him sparingly and this pattern continued under Tony Pulis, Steve Claridge and Graham Rix. Lovell then excelled in Scottish football and is currently the SPL's 10th top scorer of all time. His most recent club was Partick Thistle. He is also Eddie Howe's half brother and became engaged to singer Amy Macdonald in 2008.

Wem-ber-lee!

LUALUA, Lomana

91 apps, 19 goals (2003-2007)
Career: *Colchester United, Newcastle United, Portsmouth, Olympiacos, Al-Arabi, Olympiacos (1998-date).* Despite scoring on his debut and showing fleeting signs of brilliance, LuaLua was also extremely unpredictable during his time at the club. Disciplinary problems and a bout of malaria were interwoven with some spectacular goals (and celebrations). His son died of pneumonia while the Congelese international was living at Port Solent and this combined with reported marital differences resulted in a £4 million move to Olympiacos. He made an immediate impact and helped the club to the Greek title in his first year. Injuries again troubled him and after a long spell on the sidelines was eventually moved on to Al-Arabi in Qatar. He is now playing in Cyprus for AC Omonia.

MACKEN, Tony

10 apps, 1 goal (1975-1976)
Career: *Derby County, Portsmouth (loan), Washington Diplomats, Derby County, Walsall (1974-1981).* Irishman whose career seemed to be like one big ping pong match. He started in Southern Ireland playing for Home Farm and Waterford - two clubs that he later went on to manage. Even his two spells with Pompey were from Derby, back to Derby, to Pompey and back to Derby again!

The same pattern was repeated with two stints in America for Washington Diplomats (with one appearance for Derby in between). Walsall did manage to hold on to him for four years and almost 200 appearances before he set sail to manage a number of clubs in his homeland. He won the League Cup with Drogehdra United and was assistant manager to Ray Treacy when Shamrock Rovers won the League Championship in 1993/94.

MACKIE, Jerry

247 apps, 78 goals (1920-1928)
Career: *Motherwell, Blantyre Celtic, Portsmouth, Southampton (1928-1931).* A Scottish inside forward who played for both south Hampshire clubs in the 1920s and 1930s. Pompey became one of the founder members of the Football League Third Division for the 1920–21 season and Mackie was one of new manager, John McCartney's first signings. After his retirement from football, he became the licensee of the Regents Park Hotel in Shirley, Southampton, remaining a publican for 24 years. He later settled in Bognor Regis, where he died in 1959, a few days after his 65th birthday.

MAGUIRE, Gavin

109 apps (1988-1993)
Career: *Queens Park Rangers, Portsmouth, Newcastle United (loan), Millwall, Scarborough (loan) (1983-1994).* A gritty midfielder who won the hearts of the fans but drove his managers mad. Alan Ball had first signed him for the club as a 21 year old, but even then he had earned himself a bit of a reputation. He was taken to court for a tackle on Danny Thomas that ended the player's career, a case that resulted in an out of court settlement of around £140,000.
This should not take away from the fact that he was a great player who won full caps for his country, Wales. Sadly, as knee injury brought his own playing days to a premature end at the age of 26. He then spent some time in the United States and worked a personal trainer upon his return to England. Having decided this was not the career for him, a friend suggested that he should consider taking up hairdressing. Unlikely as it might sound bearing in mind his 'hard man' reputation, he now runs his own salon in Somerset.
7 Welsh caps.

MAHOTO, Gauthier

1 app (2009-2010)
Career: *Le Havre, Portsmouth, SC Bastia (2008-2010).* A French youngster who had earned glowing reports as a junior at Le Havre. Joined Guy Whittingham's development side but only managed one substitute appearance for the first team. Returned to France on the last day of the 2009/10 transfer window to sign for SC Bastia. However, due to mysterious administrative circumstances, it transpired that he could not play in France for three years. Subsequently he joined Greek side AEK Athens in August 2010.

MAKEL, Lee

0 apps (1998/9 loan)
Career: *Six League clubs including Pompey and five Scottish sides(1991-date).*
Joined Pompey on loan in 1999 but did not make an appearance. Still playing at the age of 37 for Swedish Division 1 Norra side Östersunds FK where he is also joint coach.

MANLEY, Malcolm

16 apps (1973-1974)
Career: *Leicester City, Portsmouth (1966-1974).* Became one of the new players drafted in thanks to John Deacon's ambition and cash injection. The plan was to create a defensive partnership between the former Leicester man and Paul Went, and this seemed to be working until Manley suffered a severed cartilage in only his 11th League game. This ended his career and he now lives back in the midlands, in Nuneaton.

MANSELL, Jack

147 apps, 11 goals (1953-1958)
Career: *Brighton, Cardiff City, Portsmouth (1948-1958).* Former Manchester United Amateur and England 'B' international. Settled in the south after being de-mobbed from the Army and played for Brighton and Cardiff before Eddie Lever paid the Welsh club £14,000 to bring him to Fratton Park. A reliable left-back, he loved to venture forward and had a cracking shot. After retiring as a player he joined the staff at Sheffield Wednesday but then coached in Greece, Turkey and Israel, where he had a spell working with the national squad. Jack has now returned to the south coast and lives in retirement is Seaford, East Sussex.

Jack Mansell
Then and now.

MANSELL, Barry

16 apps (1951-1954)
Career: *Portsmouth, Reading, Bournemouth &*
BA (1951-1957). Left back who had a
baptism of fire when he was asked to mark
Stanley Matthews in his debut in 1951. Barry
later played for Reading and Bournemouth
before emigrating to Canada. He died in 1998
aged 64.

MARCH, Zillwood 'Zac'

4 apps (1922)
Career: *Brighton & HA, Portsmouth,*
Chichester City (1920-1922). Was the oldest
surviving ex-pro at the time of his death in
1994. He was one month short of his 102nd
birthday. Played for Pompey and Brighton and
at one time turned down the opportunity to
play for Manchester United, preferring to stay
on the south coast.

MARINELLO, Peter

110 apps, 10 goals (1973-1976)
Career: *Hibernian, Arsenal, Portsmouth,*
Motherwell, Canberra City, Fulham, Phoenix
Inferno, Heart of Midlothian, Partick Thistle
(1968-1984). Was hailed as the next George
Best when he made a big money move from
Motherwell to Arsenal.

He certainly had the ability to become a top
star on the field but the attraction of the 'high
life' took its toll. He struggled to command a
regular first team slot and turned down the
offer of a new contract, preferring instead to
accept more money by signing for Pompey.
This caused a few raised eyebrows but
Chairman John Deacon was clearly delighted
to add a big name to his ambitious plans.
Sadly, the Scottish winger had a fairly
unspectacular stay. This was ultimately
brought to an end when, in an attempt to recoup some of his cash, the Chairman agreed
to sell him to Motherwell for £35,000. Later
ran a pub called Marinello's in Edinburgh but
poor decisions and mixing with the wrong
type of people saw him ultimately being
made bankrupt. He released an
autobiography called 'Fallen Idle' which
describes his rise and fall with great honesty.
He now lives in Bournemouth where he gave
up work to become full time carer for his wife.

MARINER, Paul

63 apps, 9 goals (1986-1988)
Career: *Plymouth Argyle, Ipswich Town,*
Arsenal, Portsmouth (1973-1993). English
international who only stayed one season, but
in that time helped the club win promotion
from the Second Division (in 1986/7). An
established striker who had earned his
reputation at Plymouth, Ipswich and Arsenal
was brought in from the Gunners for £150,000
and acted as the perfect foil for Mick Quinn.
This was to prove to be his league swansong
and he ended up playing in America and
Malta. Mariner set up his own management
company for footballers and briefly taught at
a Bolton school before starting a successful
coaching career in the America. He was
tempted back home by his first club,
Plymouth Argyle and became their manager
in May 2010. He has since relinquished the
role but remained on the coaching staff.

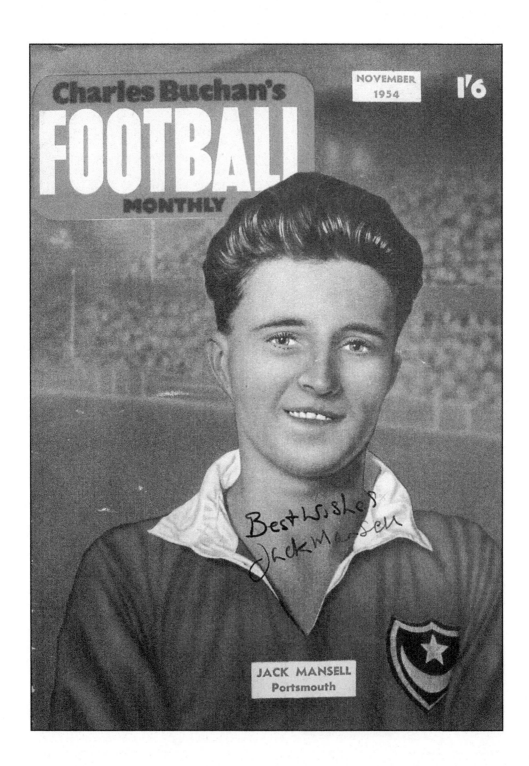

MBESUMA, Collins

4 apps (2005-2006)
Career: *Roan United, Kaizer Chiefs, Portsmouth, CS Maritimo (loan), Bursapoor, Mamelodi Sundowns, Moroka Swallows.* Nicknamed 'The Hurricane', Mbesuma was a big hit in his native South Africa and was named their Player of the Season in 2005. This was enough to persuade Alain Perrin to offer him a three year contract but from the beginning he appeared to be overweight and only made four substitute appearances for the club. He joined Turkish side Bursaspor in August 2007 but again he failed to impress and moved on to to Moroka Swallows FC the following May. He is now looking for another club following his release in 2010.

MBUYI-MUTOMBO, Andrea

0 apps (2008-2009)
Career: *Portsmouth, Zulte Waregem (loan), Standard Liege (2008-date).* A Belgian midfielder of Congelese decent who looked like a real prospect when snapped up from Belgian football. He was loaned to feeder club S.V. Zulte Waregem to gain some experience but was sent back because the club did not like his attitude. Still only 18, his contract was terminated in June 2009 and he signed a two year deal with Standard Liege.

McALINDEN, Jimmy

59 apps, 9 goals (1938-1948)
Career: *Belfast Celtic, Portsmouth, Stoke City, Southend United, Glenavon (1934-1955).* Pompey broke their transfer record to capture Irish centre forward McAlinden from Belfast Celtic in 1938. Within six months of his arrival, he was the proud owner of an FA Cup winners' medal, a souvenir that he would later display in the pub he managed after the War. He went on to manage Glenavon, Distillery, Drogheda United ad worked as a scout for Coventry City. Subsequently guided a Distillery team that included a young Martin O'Neill to a win in the 1971 Irish Cup. He died in Belfast in December 1993.

McCAFFERY, Jim

12 apps, 1 goal (1977-1979)
Career: *Nottingham Forest, Mansfield Town, Huddersfield Town, Portsmouth, Northampton (1969-1979).* Former England youth international who was brought to the club by Jimmy Dickinson 1978 from Huddersfield town for £15,000 in February 1978. The club endured relegation to the fourth division and McCaffery was allowed to join Northampton Town in the December. He went on to run a newsagents in Rothley, Leicestershire has now got one at Glenfield Hospital, Leicester.

McCANN, Albert

339 apps, 84 goals (1962-1974)
Career: *Luton Town, Coventry City, Portsmouth (1959-1973).* Powerful midfielder with an eye for goal, in fact Albie still ranks as one of the top 20 Pompey goalscorers of all time. He signed from Coventry City in 1962 and was a regular name in the starting eleven for a decade, notching up over 300 appearances in all competitions. Was awarded a testimonial in 1973 and a 22,000 crowd turned up to pay their respects and to see a West Ham side captained by Bobby Moore. A short spell in South Africa followed before returning to the area to run a newsagent's in Winter Road, Southsea. He later became a rest home proprietor in Emsworth and a regular attendee at Fratton Park.

McCLELLAN, Sid

39 apps, 10 goals (1956-1957)
Career: *Tottenham Hotspur, Portsmouth, Leyton Orient (1949-1958).* Sid joined Pompey in a £5.000 deal in 1956, featured in 39 matches and scored ten goals before joining Orient the following year. After retiring as a player he was the coach for the successful non-league side Dagenham F.C. and took them to the 1969-70 FA Amateur Cup Final. Died on 16th December 2000 aged 75.

McCLELLAND, John

150 apps, 38 goals (1962-1967)
Career: *Manchester City, Lincoln City, Queens Park Rangers, Portsmouth, Newport County (1956-1968).* It seems as though John was destined to be a footballer. His father played for Bolton Wanderers in the 1929 FA Cup final and his two older brothers had also been professionals. He made his league bow in the colours of Manchester City following his National Service and had played for Lincoln City and QPR before joining Pompey in May 1963. A speedy winger, John also bagged his fair share of goals, and Pompey turned down bids from other clubs to retain his services until a back operation in 1967/8 affected his pace. He did manage a short stay at Newport County before finally calling it a day and accepting an offer to become Pompey's maintenance officer. Having settled in Hayling Island, John later worked as a workshop technician at the local secondary school and turned out for the Pompey ex-professionals.

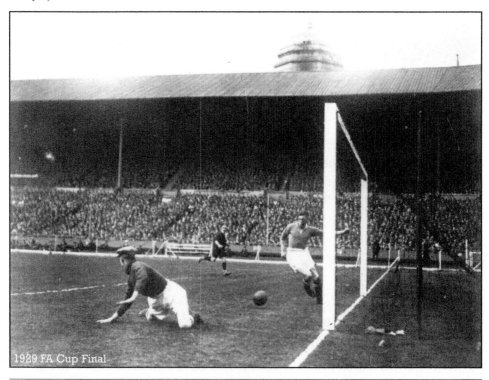

1929 FA Cup Final

McCOY, Wilf (Tim)

18 apps (1946-1948)
Career: *Portsmouth, Northampton Town, Brighton & H A (1946-1953).* Wilf, known as 'Tim' signed for the blues just after the Second World War. Although he struggled to secure a regular place he went on to become captain for Northampton Town and made almost 200 League appearances for his three clubs, the last being Brighton between 1950 and 1953. Died on 27th January 2005 after a long illness.

McFARLANE, Andy

2 apps (1991-1992)
Career: *Portsmouth, Swansea City, Scunthorpe United, Torquay United (1991-1999).* Frank Burrows was a big fan of this 6'4" striker. He snapped him up for £20,000 from non-league Cradley Town and the following year parted with the same sum as manager of Swansea to take him to the Vetch Field. Andy later played for Scunthorpe and Torquay United. He officially retired in 1999, but now, ten years on, can still be found on the muddy pitches of the south Devon League. You will be pleased to hear that his height is still being put to good use - both as a goal scorer and as the player called upon to take down the nets at the end of the match!

McGARVEY, Scott

30 apps, 6 goals (1984-1986)
Career: *Manchester United, Wolverhampton Wanderers (loan), Portsmouth, Carlisle United, Grimsby Town, Bristol City, Oldham Athletic, Wigan Athletic, Mazda, Aris Limassol, Derry City. (1980-1994).* Tipped for a big future when he broke into the first team during Ron Atkinson's first season in charge at Manchester United, but then his Old Trafford career stalled when Norman Whiteside came through. He was loaned out to Wolves and then sold to Pompey for £85,000 in July 1984. Brought in to replace Mark Hateley, he only managed a few appearances and never lived up to his star billing. Later lived in Scotland, setting up his own company, Moneystone, which sold sand to sports clubs and agricultural concerns. He then moved to Prestwich, working as a football agent and a business consultant, now manager of Manchester Maccabi.

McGHEE, Tommy

148 apps (1954-1959)
Career: *Portsmouth, Reading (1954-1959).* It is rumoured that Tommy McGee signed his first professional contract at Portsmouth Harbour station. Manager Eddie Lever was so keen to secure his signature he made a cab journey across the City to catch McGee before he caught his train back to Manchester. The right-back formed a great partnership with Jack Mansell and notched up 135 appearances over five seasons and gained a call up to the England 'B' squad. Ended his career at Reading and worked for de Havillands and British Aerospace in Hamble. Now lives in retirement in Portsmouth.

McGRATH, Lloyd

21 apps (1994-1995)
Career: *Coventry City, Portsmouth (1982-1997).* A hard-working midfielder, McGrath played for Coventry City from 1982 to 1994 and won the FA Cup in 1987. He then moved to Pompey after a time in Hong Kong. Is now a soccer coach for schools and children in Coventry and the surrounding areas.

McILWAINE, Johnny

62 apps, 5 goals (1928-1930)
Career: *Falkirk, Portsmouth, Southampton (1927-1936).* McIlwaine joined Pompey for a record fee of £5000 (including a friendly match at Fratton Park) in 1928 and helped the team avoid relegation by one point. In the 1928–29 season, he captained the team and led them to their first FA Cup Final. At the end of the following season, he was transferred to Southampton for a fee of £2650. Later became assistant manager at Southampton, and then Grimsby Town. McIlwaine remained at Blundell Park until 1948, when he left the club and opened a masseur practice in Grimsby. He remained in Grimsby for the rest of his life, dying there in April 1980, aged 75.

Photo: Ben Sutherland

McILWRAITH, Jimmy

20 apps (1978-1979)
Career: *Motherwell, Bury, Portsmouth, Bury, Halifax Town (1975-1981).* Spent a colourful year at Fratton Park during which time he received numerous bookings, was sent off, and then suspended for an incident which involved sitting on the bonnet of a car and removing an umbrella from a local pub. The club managed to sell him back to Bury for the same £15,000 that they had previously paid. Played for Halifax Town and later became a match summariser for local radio covering matches at his old club, Bury.

McLAUGHLIN, John

200 apps, 1 goal (1979-1984)
Career: *Colchester United, Swindon Town, Portsmouth, Fareham Town (1971-1983).* Former England Youth international who scored on his Pompey debut in 1979 and went on to play almost 200 games for the club but remarkably never found the net again. Frank Burrows had returned to his former club, Swindon, to pick up McLaughlin for £45,000. Over the next five years the right back gave valiant service and enjoyed two promotions before hanging up his boots at te age of 31. Played briefly for Fareham Town, then became a French polisher and now lives in Cowplain.

McLOUGHLIN, Alan

361 apps, 68 goals (1991-2000)
Career: *Manchester United, Swindon Town, Torquay United (loan), Southampton, Portsmouth, Wigan Athletic, Rochdale (1985-2002).* Former Manchester United apprentice, who despite never quite managing to break into the first team at Old Trafford, did later carve out a very successful career at both club and international level. Joined Pompey from Southampton in February 1992 for £400,000. Although he had joined from the team 'up the road', he quickly won over the crowd and went on to make over 300 appearances including the 1992 FA Cup run and become club captain. A McLoughlin goal qualified the Republic of Ireland team for the World Cup in the United States and he became the first Portsmouth player to be included in any World Cup squad since 1958. In December 1999 he was sold to Wigan Athletic for £260,000. Injuries prevented him from making a major impact and a slipped disc brought his playing days to an end. As well as being a familiar voice on local radio, Alan has also scouted for Nottingham Forest and run a soccer clinic and summer soccer schools. *Won 42 Republic of Ireland caps.*

MELLOR, Peter

146 apps (1978-1981)
Career: *Burnley, Chesterfield (loan), Fulham, Hereford United, Portsmouth, Edmonton Drillers (1969-1982).* A 20 year career was brought to a close at Fratton Park where he enjoyed popularity and success between the sticks. He had previously played for Fulham, including their 1975 FA Cup final defeat at the hands of West Ham. Mellor was at Hereford United when Jimmy Dickinson identified that his experience and bubbly personality was just what the club needed. He ended his career in America, where he now lives and coaches. He had moved over to the States in 1980 where he has also sold fireplaces, maintained gardens and swimming pools. Has been a staff coach with the United States Soccer Federation since 1992 and in February 2010 was appointed United Soccer Leagues National Technical Director. *Player of the season in 1979.*

The ball hits the back of the net during a match in 1951

MELLOWS, Mick

210 apps, 20 goals (1973-1978)
Career: *Sutton United, Reading, Winchester City, Wycombe Wanderers, Portsmouth (1965-1978).* Former England Amateur international who trained to become a teacher before deciding to turn professional. He asked Pompey for a trial and was immediately recruited. Occupying a berth on te left side of midfield, he played consistently over the next five years and won the Player of the Year award in 1975. He now lives in Portsmouth where he is now Pompey's assistant Chaplain. A devout Christian, Mick also runs 'Faith and Football' with fellow ex-Blues Linvoy Primus and Darren Moore.
Player of the season in 1975.

MENDES, Pedro

68 apps, 5 goals (2005-2009)
Career: *Vitória de Guimarães, Felgueiras (loan), Porto, Tottenham Hotspur, Portsmouth, Rangers, Sporting CP (1998-date).* A member of the 2008 FA Cup winning who joined the club in 2006 in a joint deal that included Noe Pamarot and Sean Davis. He was instrumental in helping to stave off relegation in his first season and became one of the most popular players of the time.

Only months after the glorious day at Wembley he was sold to Rangers for a fee in the region of £3 million. In January 2010, Mendes joined Sporting CP in a deal worth £1.5m. He scored his first goal for the club in a win over Everton in the Europa League.

Mick Mellows (centre)

MERSON, Paul

48 apps, 12 goals (2002-2003)
Career: *Arsenal, Brentford (loan), Middlesbrough, Aston Villa, Portsmouth, Walsall, Tamworth (1985-2006).* Although Merse only played 48 games in all competitions, he did more than enough to win the hearts of the Fratton faithful. He had been a star for Arsenal and England, winning 21 full international caps before Pompey snapped him up on a free transfer from Aston Villa in 2002. Having helped the club win promotion he felt that he was too old for the Premiership and opted instead for a move to Walsall, which was closer to his West Midlands home. He later played one game for Tamworth but is now a regular pundit on Sky Sports, and can be seen on Gillette Soccer Saturday. He also turns out for the England Legends side.

MEZAGUE, Valery

14 apps (2004-2005)
Career: *Montpelier, Portsmouth (loan), FC Sochaux, Le Havre (loan), Chateauroux, Vannes OC (1999-date).* Harry Redknapp gave this midfielder the chance to show what he could do in the Premiership when he brought the Cameroonian across from France on a loan deal in 2004. Having failed to break into the side, he was allowed to return there after only 14 games to join Alain Perrin at FC Sochaux-Montbéliard. Mezague is now with French Second Division side Vannes Olympique Club.

MIGLIORANZI, Stefani

42 apps, 2 goals (1998-2002)
Career: *Portsmouth, Swindon Town,(1999-date).* Born in Brazil but brought up in American, Miglioranzi ventured across the Atlantic to try and secure a professional football contract. After a trial, Alan Ball handed him a three year deal, but injuries interfered with what looked like a promising career. Despite knee problems, he did go onto make over 120 appearances for Swindon Town and is still playing today. He is back in the U.S.and turning out for Philadelphia Union.

MILKINS, John

389 apps (1960-1974)
Career: *Portsmouth, Oxford United (1961-1979).* John Milkins made his debut as a 16 year old in the club's last game in the first division but then had to wait another two years before his next appearance. Originally from Essex, the youngster joined the ground staff and lived in the hostel run by Duggie Reid. He went on to become one of the best keepers of the time and one of Pompey's most reliable players. Making almost 400 appearances in total, he once saved three penalties in a game against Notts County and was named Player of the Year in 1969. After 14 years service he played out the final part of his career at Oxford United. He ran his own sports shop at the top of Commercial Road for many years but once he had retired from te game he worked as manager for a club that owned snooker halls including the Pot Black club in Southampton. *Player of the year in 1969.*

MILLS, Lee

29 apps, 5 goals (2000-2001)
Career: *Ten league clubs including Pompey(1992-2005).* A club record buy when a £1.2 million was supposed to be paid to Bradford City in 2000. The club had difficulty keeping up the payments and were put under an FA embargo. On the pitch, Mills had problems finding the net and was fairly speedily moved on to Coventry City for a fraction of the original fee. Ironically, he did wear a Pompey shirt once more, when his new side played at Fratton Park but had were forced to wear our away kit because they had forgotten to bring their own. Mills became manager of Bridgnorth Town in the Midland Football Alliance club in May 2010.

MONCUR, John

7 apps (1988-1989)
Career: *Tottenham Hotspur, Portsmouth (loan), Swindon Town, West Ham United (1984-2003).* Borrowed from Tottenham Hotspur in 1988/9 an played seven League matches. Went on to play for Swindon Town and is now Chairman of Grays Athletic in the Isthmian League Division One North.

MONEY, Richard

21 apps (1983-1984)
Career: *Scunthorpe United, Fulham, Liverpool, Derby County (loan), Luton Town, Portsmouth, Scunthorpe United (1973-1990).* Bobby Campbell had previously been Money's manager at Fulham and was happy to pay Luton Town £50,00 to bring him to Fratton Park. Repeated injuries prevented a sustained run in the side and he joined Scunthorpe after just over two years but less than 20 games later. He became their manager in the 1990's and has since coached at Aston Villa, Coventry, Newcastle United and in Sweden. In May 1996, the former Liverpool defender was appointed manager at Walsall but has been in charge of Luton Town since October 2009.

MOORE, Darren

65 apps, 2 goals (1999-2002)
Career: *Torquay United, Doncaster Rovers, Bradford City, Portsmouth, WBA, Derby C, Barnsley (1992-date).* Moore was playing in the Premiership for Bradford City when Alan Ball agreed to pay £650,000 to add his 6ft 4'' frame to the squad. Apart from a spell on the sidelines due to an injury he was a rock in the heart of the Pompey defence for almost two years until he agreed to a £750,000 move back to the Midlands (born in Birmingham) and West Brom. Having been released by Barnsley in May 2010, he signed for current club Burton Albion. 'Bruno' is also on the PFA management committee and runs Faith and Football with Linvoy Primus and Mick Mellows.

Ray Hiron and John Milkins

MORAN, Paul

3 apps (1988-1989)
Career: *Tottenham Hotspur, Portsmouth (loan), Peterborough United (1985 - 1994).* Another Tottenham player who briefly appeared at Fratton Park on loan. By the time he retired in 1994, Moran had been employed by seven league clubs but only notched up a total of 34 games. Became a painter and decorator before securing a job with the FA.

MORGAN, Lew

47 apps (1938-1939)
Career: *Dundee, Portsmouth, Watford (1935-1947).* Scottish full back who played for various Scottish junior clubs before joining Dundee in 1931, and transferring to Pompey four years later. He was a member of the team that beat Wolverhampton Wanderers F.C. 4-1 in the 1939 FA Cup Final. After the Second World War he joined Watford, playing 50 Football League games for them before being released on a free transfer. He died in Portsmouth on 22nd September 1988 aged 77.

MORNAR, Ivica

12 apps, 1 goal (2004-2006)
Career: *Hajduk Split, Eintracht Frankfurt, Sevilla, Ourense, Standard Liege, Anderlecht, Portsmouth, Rennes (1991-2005).* Croatian international who turned down the offer of a new three deal at Anderlecht to join Pompey in January 2004. Managerial changes and injuries combined to restrict his first team opportunities. He left the club in 2006 and retired from the game completely the following year.

MORTIMORE, Charlie

1 app (1953-1954)
Career: *Aldershot, Woking, Portsmouth, Woking, Aldershot (1949-1955).*
Made one appearance, against Tottenham Hotspur, on Christmas Day 1953. He was a schoolteacher by profession and an amateur player with Woking at the time. Although he did play the occasional league game with Aldershot, he continued to teach until his retirement.

Current and former players gathered to play a charity match at Fareham in 2010

MORTIMORE, John

(Manager - May 1973 to September 1974.)
Made his name as as centre half with Chelsea
and QPR during his playing days, but it was a
manager that he achieved his greatest
triumphs. He helped Portuguese giants
Benfica win their national championship twice
and the Portuguese Cup in 1986 and 1987.
His CV also lists Real Betis, Beleneses,
Southampton and a short spell at Pompey in
his managerial credentials. Also coached at
Sunderland, Chelsea and Southampton,
where he became club president. Now retired
and living in the Romsey area.
Brother of Charlie, see above.

MUNDY, Albert

54 apps, 14 goals (1950-1954)
Career: *Portsmouth, Brighton & H A,
Aldershot (1950-1960).* The scouts started to
watch this slightly built forward while he was
working for a timber merchant and turning
out for Gosport County. Albert was offered a
trial at Fratton Park and signed an amateur
contract in 1951. Competition for places with
the likes of Duggie Reid and Ike Clarke
meant that his opportunities were fairly
limited. It took a move to Brighton in 1953
before his career really took off. He managed
to bag 87 goals in 166 matches while at the
Goldstone Ground. His name can also be
found in the record books to testify that he
scored one of the fastest goals (6 seconds) for
his last club, Aldershot. He returned to
Gosport in 1960 to become their
player/manager and later drove lorries for
fellow ex-Pompey player Dennis Edwards,
who ran a refrigerated food business in the
city.

MUNKS, David

149 apps, 2 goals (1969-1974)
Career: *Sheffield United, Portsmouth,
Swindon, Exeter City (1965-1975).* Sheffield
born defender won two England Youth caps
while with home town club Sheffield United.
Joined Pompey in the 1969 close season and
became a popular first team regular. Was
named Player of the Year in 1971 but found
himself out of favour when John Deacon took
over the club and started to bring in his own
choice of players. One by one anyone that
had not been purchased by the Chairman

were allowed to leave the club and David was
transferred to Swindon Town in 1973. His
career was brought to an end by injury in
1976, while playing for Exeter City. Now lives
in Bedhampton and has managed leisure
centres and swimming pools for Southampton
City Council, the Moneyfield Social Club for
two years and then a tile showroom in Hedge
End.
Player of the season in 1971.

MUNTARI, Sulley

33 apps, 5 goals (2007-2008)
Career: *Udinese, Portsmouth, Internazionale
(2002-date).* A Ghanaian footballer who,
despite falling out with his team-mates and
the footballing authorities, recently helped his
home country reach the quarter finals of the
World Cup in South Africa. He currently plays
for Serie A club Inter Milan, having joined the
Italian giants from Pompey for a reported €16
million in July 2008. This represented an
impressive 'paper profit' after only one
season on the south coast. However, it was
quite a season. He was outstanding and
played a significant role in the winning of the
FA Cup.
*Muntari was voted as an All-Star Player
during the 2008 African Cup of Nations
Tournament in Ghana.*

MURRAY, Shaun

45 apps, 2 goals (1990-1993)
Career: *Portsmouth, Scarborough, Bradford City, Notts County, Kettering Town (1989-2003).* Shaun was a initially a junior at Tottenham Hotspur but signed for Pompey in 1989 for £100,000. He played just 45 games in more than three seasons and moved north to play for Scarborough, Bradford City and Notts County before finishing his career at Kettering Town and finally Hinckley United. Most recently, he turned out for Notts County in the 2010 Midlands Masters five-a-side tournament.

MUSSELWHITE, Paul

Junior (1988)
Career: *Scunthorpe United, Port Vale, Hull City, Scunthorpe United (1988-2006).* Goalkeeper and former Pompey youngster who went on to play over 600 league matches for a number of northern clubs. He is now Lincoln City's goalkeeping coach.

MVUEMBA, Arnold

32 apps, 2 goals (2006-2009)
Career: *Stade Rennais, Portsmouth, FC Lorient (1999-date).* French midfielder Mvuemba was signed on loan from Stade Rennais in January 2007 with an option to complete a permanent deal He made his debut against Blackburn Rovers the following month and signed a three-year contract in the July. He did score against VfL Wolfsburg in the UEFA Cup but was released by the club in August 2009. Arnold now plays for FC Lorient in his home country.

MWARUWARI, Benjani

77 apps, 19 goals (2005-2008)
Career: *Jomo Cosmos, Grasshopper (loan), Auxerre, Portsmouth, Manchester City, Sunderland (loan) (2002-date).* Zimbabwean striker signed from Auxerre in January 2006 and the transfer later came under scrutiny during the Stevens enquiry into financial wrongdoings. It took a while for Benjani to get going but by the time he left for Manchester City he was regularly scoring goals including a hat-trick in the 7–4 win over Reading, which broke the record for the most number of goals scored in a Premier League match. Sven-Göran Eriksson's agreed to pay up to

£7.5m in January 2008 to take him to Maine Road. The transfer was not completed until the following month because the player had apparently missed two planes to Manchester, having fallen asleep at the airport. This meant that he had arrived too late to sign the forms before the midnight deadline. Despite the sizeable fee, Benjani has never re-captured the scintillating form shown in his latter days at Fratton Park and has subsequently been loaned out to Sunderland and now plays for Blackburn Rovers.

MYERS, Andy

8 apps (1999-2000)
Career: *Chelsea, Bradford City, Portsmouth (loan), Colchester United, Brentford (1991-2005).* Myers began his career with Chelsea, and featured in the sides which won the FA Cup in 1997, and the League Cup and Cup Winners' Cup in 1998. He was sold to Bradford City in 1999 for £800,000. Following that, he had a short stay at Pompey on loan. Tony Pulis wanted to sign him permanently, but Bradford were holding out for £600,000, which was double what Pompey were prepared to pay. He later played for Colchester United and then Brentford, who released him at the end of the 2004–05 season. Has business interests that include a company which supplies air conditioning and electrical blinds and curtains, and another which supplies high end entertainment equipment in houses, clients are said to include John Terry. His business partners are ex-Chelsea players Jody Morris and Michael Duberry.

NDEBE-NLOME, Berlin

Career: *KVC Westerlo, Portsmouth, Crawley Town (2006-2008).* A former Cameroonian U20 international, Ndebe-Nlome came to Fratton Park on trial and played in several pre-season friendlies. He was eventually offered a contract at the club and received a work permit, but signed for Crawley Town on a short-term deal in November 2007 without having made a first team appearance. He didn't last much longer there and was released after only six weeks. In July 2009 he was offered a chance to impress on trial at Swindon Town F.C.and appeared in two pre-season friendlies but struggled to make the necessary impact to earn a longer stay.

NEIL, Pat

11 apps, 3 goals (1955-6 and 1962-3)
Career: *Portsmouth, Wolves, Portsmouth (1954-1965).* Pat's story is one that many schoolboys can only dream about. Despite only making a handful of league appearances, he played with some of the footballing greats and also gained a degree from Cambridge University. As a youngster, he helped out in the offices at Fratton Park during his school holidays and was occasionally allowed to join in with the training on the pitch. Imagine his surprise when an ankle injury to Peter Harris meant that he was called up to join the first team for a match at Huddersfield. As a result he became Pompey's youngest ever debutant and had to juggle school work with playing duties for the rest of the season. Due to a possible mix up, Pat left the club and joined Wolves the following summer. Here he shared a dressing room (and the bus journey to and from training) with the great Billy Wright. A career in teaching beckoned but he continued to play amateur football at the highest level. His last post was as head teacher at Midhurst intermediate school and since retiring has been extremely active, not least with the running of the Portsmouth former Players' Association.

NEILL, Warren

260 apps, 5 goals (1988-1995)
Career: *Queens Park Rangers, Portsmouth, Watford. (1980-1996).* Neill made his league debut for QPR debut against Chelsea in 1980 and went on to play 181 league games scoring 3 goals. He played in the FA Cup Final replay in 1982, was part of the Second Division Championship team in 1983 and a member of the 1986 Milk Cup final team. He moved to Pompey in 1988 for a fee of £110,000 to fill the gap left by Kenny Swain's departure. Despite a wobbly spell during John Gregory's time as manager, Warren managed to win the fans over and made the right back spot his own for six seasons. He was part of the team that reached the 1992 FA Cup semi final, but was one of three players to miss his kick as in the penalty shootout. Ironically, he was invited to join the QPR coaching staff by manager John Gregory towards the end of the 2006/07 season. initially this was on a temporary basis, but the deal was made permanent in June 2007. In January 2008 Neill joined Luton Town as assistant to Mick Harford, but was released from his position in November 2008. Now believed to be driving a cab in London.

Pat Neil

NEWHOUSE, Aidan

6 apps, 1 goal (1994-1995)
Career: *Chester City, Wimbledon, Portsmouth (loan), Fulham, Swansea City, Brighton (1988-1999).* A former England youth international who spent a month on loan at Fratton Park. Newhouse was registered to Wimbledon at the time and had appeared for them in the top flight. Jim Smith decided against parting with the required £300,000 for a permanent move and he eventually joined Fulham instead. After retiring from football, he became a maths teacher and currently works in Rainhill High School.

NEWMAN, Ron

116 apps, 24 goals (1956-1961)
Career: *Portsmouth, Leyton Orient, Crystal Palace Palace, Gillingham (1954-1965).* Ron Newman was born in Fareham and served Pompey well as a bustling forward in the late 1950's but it was in the United States where he became a massive star. Having accepted an offer to coach Dallas Tornado in 1969, he went on to establish himself as arguably the most successful coach in the history of American soccer. Over the next 30 years his teams won all of the major titles including the ASL, NASL, and the indoor league championship 10 times with San Diego. He has been inducted into the National Soccer Hall of Fame, Dallas Walk of Fame, Atlanta Soccer Hall of Fame and was granted the 'Key of the City' in San Diego and Fort Lauderdale. Despite the fame and glory he still manages to come back to catch up with his old playing buddies at Fratton Park.

NEWTON, Adam

5 apps. (1999-2000)
Career: *West Ham United, Portsmouth (loan), Notts County (loan), Leyton Orient (loan), Peterborough United, Brentford, Luton Town (1998-date).* An English-born Saint Kittitian and Nevisian professional footballer, who had a loan stint at Fratton Park in 1999. He began his career as a youth player with West Ham United, where he was a member of their FA Youth Cup winning squad in 1999 and has been a member of the Saint Kitts and Nevis national football team since 2004, even though he had previously represented England at Under 21 level. Adam has been playing for Luton Town in the Conference since August 2009.

NIEMI, Antti

Career: *HJK, Copenhagen, Rangers, Heart of Midlothian, Southampton, Fulham, Portsmouth*
Finnish ex-Southampton goalkeeper signed by Harry Redknapp as back up for David James. The former international had been Fulham's first choice stopper until 2008 when he retired from the game. Having agreed to help, he came and went without making a first team appearance but with his bank account nicely swollen. It is claimed that he earned £450,000 for his eight months at the club. On 2nd March 2010 Niemi joined Finland's national team as a goalkeeping coach.

NIGHTINGALE, Luke

51 apps, 8 goals (1998-2001)
Career: *Portsmouth, Swindon Town (loan), Southend United, Weymouth, Bognor Regis Town, Havant & Waterlooville, Bognor Regis Town (1998-date).* Nightingale made his league bow as an 18 year old having started the season in the youth team. His goalscoring exploits for the reserves ensured a rapid rise to the first team and he bagged another two on his debut against West Brom. He has since played for Southend United, Swindon Town, Worthing and Bognor Regis. In his opening season with Bognor Regis Town (2004-05) he was the Conference South's leading scorer with 28 goals. Joined Havant & Waterlooville in 2008 but returned to Bognor in January 2010. Luke lives in Southsea and earns his living as a kitchen and bathroom fitter.

NOAKES, Alf

14 apps (1962-1964)
Career: *West Ham, Crystal Palace, Portsmouth, Tunbridge Wells Rangers (1950-1963)*. Having gained promotion to the second division in 1962, manager George Smith returned to his former club to snap up left-back Noakes. Described as a tough, chirpy character he had made over 200 first team appearances for Palace and helped them gain promotion to the Third Division in 1961. His stay at Fratton Park was less successful and he was released on a free transfer in June 1964. Alf passed away in October 2005 at the age of 72.

O'BRIEN, Andy

37 apps (2005-2007)
Career: *Bradford City, Newcastle United, Portsmouth, Bolton Wanderers (1996-date)*. English-born Irish centre back who won 26 caps for Republic of Ireland between 2001 and 2006, and was a member of Ireland's 2002 World Cup squad. O'Brien was Alain Perrin's first signing when he paid Newcastle United £2 million for his services and he established himself in the first team until an injury ended his run. Upon recovery, he found it hard to regain his place due to the strong partnership that had developed between Sol Campbell and Linvoy Primus in his absence. This ultimately led to his departure and he eventually joined Bolton Wanderers in August 2007. His time at the Reebok has been much happier, he was appointed captain and named as the club's Player of the Season in 2008.

O'CALLAGHAN, Kevin

100 apps, 17 goals
Career: *Millwall, Ipswich Town, Portsmouth, Southend United* 'Cally' helped Pompey back into the top flight in 1986/7. He formed part of a deadly striking formation that also included Mick Quinn, Paul Mariner and Vince Hilaire. Although he was an effective winger and holder of 21 international caps, he may well be best remembered for his role in the 1981 film Escape to Victory, where he took on the role of goalkeeper 'Hatch'. In the company of Sylvester Stallone. Michael Caine, Bobby Moore and Pele, 'Hatch' saved a penalty in the last minute of the match against the Nazis to secure a victory for the Allies' side.

He may not have made much of an impression at Fratton Park, but
Emmanuel Olisadebe's wedding was headline news in Poland.

O'CONNELL, Brendan

0 apps (1985-1986)
Career: *Portsmouth, Exeter City, Burnley, Barnsley, Charlton Athletic, Wigan Athletic (1985-1998).* Former Pompey youngster who made 451 appearances and scored 79 goals in the League for Exeter City, Burnley, Huddersfield Town, Barnsley, Charlton Athletic and Wigan Athletic. He was forced to retire from playing because of a blood clot in his leg and went on to coach Wigan Athletic's youth and reserve teams. Played briefly for Rossendale United in the North West Counties League and in 2003 became player/assistant manager of Northwich Victoria.

OLISADEBE, Emmanauel

2 apps (2005-2006)
Career: *Jasper United, Polonia Warszawa, Panathinaikos, Portsmouth, Skoda Xanthi (loan), APOP Kinyras Peyias, Henan Construction (1995-date).* A Nigerian striker and a former Polish international who had broken the record for the greatest number of goals scored by a Polish player in a single World Cup qualifying tournament and was a contender for the FIFA World Footballer of the Year 2001. He joined Pompey's battle against relegation in 2005 on a 'pay as you play' deal. However, this did not make him rich - he only managed two games before leaving for the Greek island of Xanthi. Olisadebe has since played in Cyprus for Kinyras Peyia FC and in the Chinese Super League with Henan Construction. 12 goals in his first season in China meant that he was the country's second highest scorer and he was nominated for the Most Valuable Player of the year award for two consecutive seasons, being pipped into second place on both occasions.

OLSZAR, Sebastian

1 app (2003-2004)
Career: *Portsmouth, Coventry City (loan), Polonia Warszawa, Górnik Zabrze, Polonia Warszawa, Zagłębie Sosnowiec, Piast Gliwice (2000-date).* Polish forward whose brief stay included one first team appearance before trying his luck at Coventry City. His English experience proved to be short lived and he quickly returned home, where he has since played for a number of clubs. He has been on the books at Ruch Chorzów. since early 2010.

O'NEIL, Gary

193 apps, 17 goals (2000-2008)
Career: *Portsmouth, Walsall (loan), Cardiff City (loan), Middlesbrough (1999-date).* Made his debut as a 16 year old in January 2000 but had to be patient over the next few years as a succession of managers only used him as a bit-part player. Things finally changed in 2001/2 when his reputation continued to grow and earned him a call up to join the England Under 20 squad and to captain the side in the 2003 FIFA World Youth Championship. When Technical director Velimir Zajec took over a temporary manager he made O'Neil a regular in the Pompey midfield and his consistently impressive performances led to a £5 million bid from then European Champions Liverpool. Gary was named Player of the Year in 2006 but was sold the following season to Middlesbrough in August 2007 for a fee of about £5 million.

OSMOND, Colin

1 app (1957-1958)
Career: *Portsmouth, Poole Town (1957-1958).* Made one appearance at centre half as a 20 year old but is remembered by Poole Town fans as one of their all time greats.

PACK, Roy

105 apps, 1 goal (1966-1969)
Career: *Arsenal, Portsmouth, Oxford United (1965-1969).* London born Pack was spotted by Arsenal as a youngster and did make one appearance for the Gunners' first team. George Smith brought him to Fratton Park as a 19 year old with potential and the right back berth became his own for the next three seasons. An injury sustained in an FA Cup tie against Fulham ended his run and he was forced to retire from the game. In recent years he has been investigating corruption in football. Following the death of former West Brom and England Striker Jeff Astle, Roy as Compliance Officer with a group called ExPro lobbied the government in the hope that they might agree that injuries sustained during a career in soccer should be treated the same way as other industries that pay our pensions for industrial disease. He claimed to have built up a dossier on 600 players who had suffered brain damage, Alzheimers or dementia as a result of playing the sport.

PAMAROT, Noe

80 apps, 5 goals (1999-2009)
Career: *Martigues, Nice, Portsmouth (loan), Tottenham Hotspur, Portsmouth, Hercules (1997-date).* Frenchman Pamarot was part of the deal that bought Sean Davis and Pedro Mendes from Spurs in 2006 for a combined fee of £7.5 million. In fact, this represented a return to the club as he had previously had a loan spell at Fratton Park in the 1999-2000 season. Although he notched up 80 appearances in his three year stay, he was released at the end of his contract in 2008. Rather appropriately for a strong defender, he joined Spanish team Hercules.

PANOPOULOS, Michael

58 apps, 7 goals (1999-2002)
Career: *Portsmouth, Dunfermline Athletic, Aris Thessaloniki, South Melbourne, AO Kerkyra, Oakleigh Cannons (1993-2007).* Mike Panopoulos is an Australian-Greek who gave up the Greek sunshine to sign for the Blues in August 1999. The £1 million fee was a record for the club at the time and he stayed for the next three years. In December 2001 Panopoulos moved on loan to Dunfermline F.C. in the Scottish Premier League and left permanently shortly thereafter. He transferred to South Melbourne FC and then made a move to Greece with Kerkyra F.C. Has since returned to Australia and works as Head Soccer Coach of Wesley College.

PARKER, Cliff

258 apps, 63 goals (1938-1950)
Career: *Denaby United, Doncaster Rovers, Portsmouth, Denaby United (1931-1950).* Cliff earned his place in the history books and Pompey fans' hearts with two goals in the FA Cup final victory over Wolves in 1939. An old fashioned outside left, he ploughed up and down the wing either side of WW2, but rather more unusually, throughout the war years as well. With the added competition for places provided by Peter Harris and Jack Froggatt his outings reduced as the years progressed but he remained with the club as a player until 1953 when he became a scout. Was assistant trainer between 1954 and 1957 but retained his links for many years after by turning out for the ex-professionals side. His latter years were spent in retirement on the Isle of Wight and he died there in January 1983.

Cliff Parker

PASANEN, Petri

16 apps (2003-2004)
Career: *Kuusysi Lahti, Lahti, Hameenlinna (loan), Ajax, Portsmouth, Werder Bremen (1996-date).* Finnish defender, who fell out of favour at Ajax in 2003–04 and spent the second half of the season on loan at Pompey. Harry Redknapp was interested in buying Pasanen at the end of the season, but claimed Ajax's asking price was too high. The Finn was then signed by reigning German champions Werder Bremen in the summer of 2004. He has since helped them to a top three finish in the Bundesliga and the second round of the Champions League. A regular for the Finnish national team, he has also played in Finland futsal national team, where he has six caps and two goals. (Futsal is an indoor version of the game played with a smaller ball.)

PEARSON, Richard

4 apps, 1 goals (1952-1953)
Career: *Portsmouth (1952/3)*
Former England Boys international played four League games in 1952-3 before joining up with ex-blues Charlie Dore, Johnny Beale and Brian Edwards at Guildford City. He is now retired but enjoyed a full working life as a fireman at Wisley Airport and more recently in security for a cork and rubber firm in Surrey.

PELE

Career: *Vitoria, Internationale, Porto, Portsmouth (loan), Real Valladolid (loan). (2006-date).* Vitor Hugo Gomes Passos, nicknamed Pelé is a Portuguese Under 21 international midfielder who never broke through into the first team during his time at the club. He left in 2009 and currently plays for Real Valladolid on loan from Porto.

PENK, Harry

10 apps, 2 goals (1955-1957)
Career: *Wigan Athletic, Portsmouth, Plymouth Argyle, Southampton (1955-1963).* Tiny winger who only measured 5'4" in his socks. Signed from his home-town club Wigan Athletic in 1955, Harry struggled to dislodge regular first-teamers Peter Harris and Jackie Henderson but later in his career made more of a name for himself at Southampton. Has worked at Husband's Shipyard in the city but has suffered two brain tumours.

PENNANT, Jermaine

14 apps (2008-2009)
Career: *Notts County, Arsenal, Birmingham City, Liverpool, Portsmouth (loan), Real Zaragoza (1998-date).* Former loanee Pennant has regularly hit the headlines during an explosive career. As a 15 year old he went from Notts County trainee to Arsenal's youngest ever first team player in a record £2 million move and scored a hat-trick on his full debut. He played 13 games at Pompey but after a spell with Real Zaragoza in Spain he returned home to play for Stoke City.

PERICARD, Vincent

49 apps, 10 goals (2002-2006)
Career: *Saint-Etienne, Juventus, Portsmouth, Stoke City, Carlisle United, Swindon Town (1999-date)*. French Under 21 international Péricard initially moved to Fratton Park on loan in 2002 and scored on his debut in a 2–0 win over Nottingham Forest. He impressed enough to earn a permanent switch in July 2003, having scored nine times in 32 games as Pompey won the Division One title. His stay lasted until 2006 when he was released and agreed to join Stoke City on a free transfer. On 24 August 2007 Pericard was sentenced to four months in prison after being found guilty of perverting the course of justice. He had lied about being the driver of a car caught speeding at 103 mph near Plymouth. Now plays for Swindon Town.

PERON, Jeff

54 apps, 3 goals (1998-2000)
Career: *Strasbourg, Lens, AS Monaco, Caen, Walsall, Portsmouth, Wigan Athletic (1990's)*. It was a surprise when Alan Ball paid Walsall £150,000 for the Frenchman, who was 32 at the time. He had only played one season in England, although he had been named as the midlanders' Player of the Year in that year. Alan Ball's judgement proved to be well founded and Jeff became a regular starter and popular with the fans. A disagreement with the manager led to his hasty departure less than two years later. Moved to Wigan Althletic before being released and returning home to France.

PERRETT, Russell

80 apps, 2 goals (1995-1999)
Career: *AFC Lymington, Portsmouth, Cardiff City, Luton Town, Bournemouth (1994-2008)*. Became a bit of a 'come-back kid' when he signed a pro deal in 1995 having initially been released by the club. Russell was part of an impressive youth side that contained Darren Anderton, Andy Awford, and Kit Symons but unlike his team-mates, but his path to the first team was via a stint at his local club Lymington. He notched up 80 appearances before Frank Burrows took him to Cardiff City for £10,000 in 1999. He played for Luton Town and Bournemouth before retiring in May 2008.

PERRIN, Alain

(Manager between April and November 2005.) 'Reggie' Perrin had started out as junior coach to Arsene Wenger at AC Nancy in the early 1980's and went on to make a name for himself as a successful manager in his home country, France. As boss of Olympique Marseilles and subsequently he once broke the French transfer record to capture one Didier Dogba. He also took charge at Marseille, had a spell in in the United Arab Emirates and eight months at Fratton Park. Relegation was avoided in his first season but his sacking came only a few months later as his side slid down the table. His career since has shown a remarkable upturn in fortune. He won the French Cup with FC Sochaux in 2007, won the league and then retained the French cup in his first season as manager of Olympique Lyonnais. He is now in charge of Alkhor SC in Qatar.

PERRIN, Steve

35 apps, 4 goals (1980-1981)
Career: *Wycombe W, Crystal Palace, Plymouth Argyle, Portsmouth, Hillingdon Borough, Northampton Town, Wycombe W (1976-1982).* Was a member of the side that won promotion out of the old Fourth Division in 1979-80 and could slot comfortably into the side as centre forward or in the heart of the defence. Steve became a school teacher after retiring from the game but still played in non-league soccer. After ten years as a deputy head at a local primary school, he was appointed Headmaster at Bushey Heath Primary School, in Hertfordshire.

PETHICK, Robbie

218 apps, 3 goals (1993-1999)
Career: *Weymouth, Portsmouth, Bristol Rovers, Brighton, Havant & Waterlooville (1992-2006).* Devon born Pethick was working for the local Water Authority and playing non-league football for Saltash when he got his first break with Weymouth. It was while playing for the Dorset club that Jim Smith spotted his potential and parted with £100,000 to bring him to Fratton Park. The Bald Eagle's faith was repaid over the next six years when Robbie put in consistent performances and clocked up over 200 league starts. Pethick also played for Bristol Rovers and Brighton before retiring from football in 2006. Now lives in Cowplain and works as a driver for a window company.

PETTEFER, Carl

3 apps (2000-2002)
Career: *Portsmouth, Exeter City (loan), Southend United, Oxford United, Bournemouth, Bognor Regis Town, AFC Totton (1999-date).* Midfielder who spent five years on the books and made a fleeting visit to first team action in the early noughties. He has since turned out for Exeter City (on loan from Pompey), Oxford United, Bournemouth, Bognor Regis and has been at AFC Totton since 2008.

PETTERSON, Andy

34 apps (1998-2001)
Career: *Swindon Town, Charlton Athletic, Portsmouth, West Bromwich Albion, Brighton, plus numerous others on loan (1988-date).*

Much travelled Australian keeper who added Pompey to his long list of clubs in 1998. He had been Charlton Athletic's first choice keeper but the arrival of Sasa Ilic meant he was free to move to Fratton Park as cover for Alan Knight. Later had brief stops at a further seven clubs (plus Derry City across the water) but remarkably only a further eleven league appearances in total. On his Walsall debut Petterson conceded six goals and played for Notts County before catching the plane back to Australia. Now plays in Perth for semi professional outfit ECU Joondalup.

PHILLIPS, John

81 apps (1955-1959)
Career: *Portsmouth, Worcester City (1955-1960).* Local boy, Johnny Phillips, spent most of his Pompey career involved in relegation battles and had to endure the pain of the drop in 1959, the year before his departure. He was allowed to join Worcester City, where he linked up with fellow Pompey old boy Bill Thompson and Andy Awford's father, Terry. When George Smith was appointed manager, he tried to lure Johnny back but Worcester held out for a fee which was beyond the reach of the limited Pompey coffers. He did finally return to the city, but as a painter and decorator rather than as a player. Now retired but still an active member of the Pompey Ex-Professionals Association.

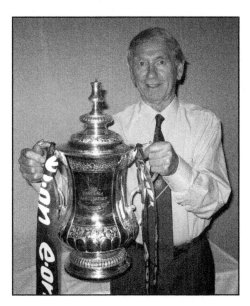

PHILLIPS, Len

271 apps, 55 goals (1946-1956)
Career: *Royal Marines, Portsmouth, Poole Town, Chelmsford City, Bath City (1946-1954).* Phillips was serving in the Royal Marines and had previously been involved in the D-Day landings when Pompey offered him a trial. (A Corporal serving with him in the marines had written to the club suggesting that he had the ability to make the grade.) Although the war had meant that he was a late starter, there is no doubt that the years that followed saw him become one of the best players of his era. Playing as an inside-left and later as a wing-half, he earned three full England caps and the respect of supporters of both the national side and his only league club. Len had played his part in the two consecutive league title wins and played over 250 games before an injury sustained in an England practice match ended his career in 1956. He went on to play non-league football for Poole Town, Chelmsford City and Bath City, then worked as a lathe operator at the De Havilland works in Portsmouth. Stayed in the area to enjoy his retirement.

PHILLIPS, Martin

29 apps, 1 goal (1998-2000)
Career: *Exeter City, Manchester City, Portsmouth, Bristol Rovers (loan), Plymouth Argyle, Torquay United (1994-2007).* Alan Ball was a big fan of Martin Phillips having managed him at Exeter City, Manchester City and then being responsible for bringing him to Fratton Park for £100,000 in 1998. Having failed to establish himself, he returned to his roots to play for Plymouth Argyle and Torquay United before being forced to retire from the game due to suffering chronic fatigue syndrome.

PICKETT, Reg

128 apps, 3 goals (1949-1957)
Career: *Weymouth, Portsmouth, Ipswich Town, Stevenage Town (1949-1962).* Born in India, Reg Pickett was brought up in the Reading area and had resisted an offer to join Dumfermline while the family were stationed in Scotland to join Weymouth in the Western League. It was during this time that he came to Pompey's attention and resulted in a £750 transfer to the current First Division champions. His preferred position was wing-half but during his eight years at the club, he played in almost every outfield position. In 1957 he joined Ipswich Town who were managed by Alf Ramsey at the time and as captain of the Suffolk club, led them to the Second Division Championship in 1961. After a couple of years playing non-league football Reg returned to the Portsmouth area and worked at the dockyard until his retirement at the age of 60. He then moved over to the Isle of Wight to live in St Helens.

Len Phillips with his Hall of Fame trophy

PIPER, Norman

355 apps, 57 goals (1970-1978)
Career: *Plymouth Argyle, Portsmouth (1965-1978).* An England Under 23 international whose £40,000 transfer from Plymouth Argyle equalled the club's existing record, which had been set by his former Plymouth team-mate Mike Trebilcock's move from Everton. Despite constant fear that he would be snapped up by a First division club, he played over 350 games over the next eight years and added more Under 23 caps to his trophy cabinet. Time was called in 1978 when Ian St John shuffled the team and Norman was replaced by the only other Piper to play for the club - his namesake Steve had been brought in from Brighton. At this point he accepted a contract to play for Fort Lauderdale and is still in America today. He now is a coach for Carlsbad Lightning in Southern California. *England Under 23 international*

PIPER, Steve

30 apps, 2 goals (1977-1978)
Career: *Brighton, Portsmouth (1972-1978).* A £25,000 capture from Brighton & Hove Albion. Unfortunately a knee injury sustained in his first season at Fratton Park effectively ended Piper's career, although he did later manage to play at non-league level for Worthing. Settled in Southwick, West Sussex where he became an insurance and mortgage broker.

PITT, Courtney

41 apps, 3 goals (2001-2002)
Career: *Portsmouth, Luton Town (loan), Coventry City (loan), Oxford United, Boston United, Cambridge United, York City (loan) (2001-date).* Former Chelsea youth player who had worked under Graham Rix at Stamford Bridge and jumped at the prospect of first team football when his former coach became Pompey boss. Signed non-contract terms with Weymouth in September 2010

POINTER, Ray

165 apps, 31 goals (1966-1971)
Career: *Burnley, Bury, Coventry City, Portsmouth, Havant & Waterlooville (1957-1975).* England international who made over 400 league appearances for Burnley, Bury, Coventry, and Pompey. He won three England caps and a League Winner's medal with Burnley before finding himself at Fratton Park during the latter stages of his career. Although mainly employed in a midfield Role, he did bag 31 goals and won the first ever Player of the Year trophy. Later coached at Burnley, Bury and Blackpool, where he now lives in retirement.

POLLOCK, Maitland

65 apps, 11 goals (1976-1978)
Career: *Nottingham Forest, Walsall, Burton Albion, Luton Town, Portsmouth, Queen of the South (1970-1977).* Pollock had played in the same Scottish schoolboy side as Graham Souness and had made four league starts when signed from Luton Town in March 1974. He was an ever present in the fight against relegation in 1976/7 but was released the following year when the club failed to avoid the drop for a second time. He returned to Scotland to play for Queen of the South. Still lives north of the border and has taken his coaching badges but prefers to spend his time on the golf course.

Photo: Tobreatheasone

POOM, Mart

7 apps (1995-1996)
Career: *Portsmouth, Flora Tallinn (loan), Derby County, Sunderland, Arsenal, Watford (1988-2009).* Estonian football goalkeeper who won 120 caps was brought to the club by Jim Smith for a £200,000 fee but was unable to dislodge Alan Knight. In November 2003, the Estonian Football Association named him as the country's greatest player of the last 50 years. Became goalkeeping coach at Arsenal and for his national side.

PORTWOOD, Cliff

106 apps, 30 goals (1964-1969)
Career: *Preston North End, Port Vale, Grimsby Town, Portsmouth, Durban United (1955-1969).* Born in Salford, Cliff Portwood was an apprentice at Preston and acted as Tom Finney's understudy as progressed towards first team football. Having established himself as a lethal goalscorer in his own right

during spells with Bury, George Smith paid £4,000 to bring him south. He was top scorer in 1964/5 and bagged two goals in Pompey's first ever game shown on BBC's Match of the Day programme. In 1969 he decided to moved over to South Africa rather than play in the lower divisions in England. It was here that he won a talent contest that entitled him to a recording contract in Australia. Portwood moved to Melbourne and embarked on what would prove to be a successful new career as a singer. Sales of his songs earned him Gold Discs and regular TV appearances until he returned to England in the 1980's. Ran the 'Gentleman Jim' in Alton before jetting off again, this time to America. A lung condition forced him to give up his singing career in Florida and he now lives back in Farnham

POWELL, Darryl

170 apps, 23 goals (1988-1995)
Career: *Portsmouth, Derby Co, Birmingham C, Sheff Wed, Nottingham Forest (1989-2005).* The son of a Reggae musician who played Jamaica in France 98 where they were appropriately nicknamed the Reggae Boyz. He was given his first start by Jim Smith in 1988 and went to make over 350 league appearances for five English clubs. He also represented England in Beach Soccer but now runs his own business as a licensed football agent, Paramount Sports Management Ltd in Sutton Coldfield.

POWER, Lee

3 apps (1993-1994)
Career: *Norwich City, Portsmouth (loan), Bradford City, Peterborough United, Dundee, Hibernian, Ayr United, Plymouth Argyle, Halifax Town (1990-2000).* Capped by Republic of Ireland at Youth, Under-21 and B level, Power played a few games on loan from Norwich City in 1993/4. Was forced to retire from the game at the age of 28 and became a football agent before setting up a sports publishing company. Became chairman of Cambridge United and then joined the board of their Conference rivals Rushden in 2008.

PRICE, Chris

21 apps (1992-1994)
Career: *Hereford United, Blackburn Rovers, Aston Villa, Blackburn Rovers, Portsmouth, Cinderford Town (1977-1996).* Was a vastly experienced full back with over 500 league appearances to his name when he put pen to paper on a £50,000 transfer from Blackburn Rovers. His time on the south coast seemed to be doomed from the start, he was sent off in his first match and then suffered an injury that ended his professional career. Price managed Newport AFC and Cinderford Town before moving to Spain in 2003 where he was involved with Charlton Athletic's European Soccer School in Torrevieja. He later emigrated to Australia.

PRIMUS, Linvoy

219 apps, 6 goals (2000-2009)
Career: *Charlton Athletic, Barnet, Reading, Portsmouth (1992-2009).* Even though Linvoy played for three other clubs, he has been adopted one of Pompey's own and become one of the club's most popular players of all time. Remarkably he did not cost a penny, having signed from Reading on a 'Bosman' free transfer. Injuries hampered his early days at Fratton Park but once he broke into the first team he became an instant hero and immediately won the Player of the Year award. The likable Londoner was forced to retire in 2009 after a long fight to recover from a further injury. His name is now immortalised in Fratton folklore and sits proudly above the old Milton End, which is now known as the Linvoy Primus Community Stand. He now splits his time between duties for the club and running his charity Faith and Football.

PRISCOTT, Tony

40 apps, 8 goals (1959-1961)
Career: *Portsmouth, Aldershot, Bournemouth, Aldershot. (1959-1971).* Diminutive winger who wrote to Pompey asking for a trial. It took over a year, and some chasing, before he was offered a contract to play for the club on the princely wage of £7 per week. He was a member of the youth team that reached the quarter final of the English Youth Cup and went on to make 40 appearances in the first team. Later played for Aldershot and Bournemouth and had a spell as manager of Ringwood. It was at Ringwood that he met up with Rod Taylor, who he had known from his Pompey days and they set up a building company which operated successfully until 1982. Christianity dramatically changed his life and he set up a church in Ringwood.

PRISKE, Brian

33 app (2005-2006)
Career: *Portsmouth, Club Brugge, Vejle Boldklub (1996-date).* A full Danish international, Alain Perrin gave him his chance in English football in 2005 but when the manager was sacked four months later, Priske was dropped by new boss Harry Redknapp. The following August he returned to Belgian football to play for Club Brugge. Still playing in his Danish homeland for Vejle Boldklub.

PROBERT, William

245 apps (1920's)
Career: *Worksop Town, Portsmouth, Southends United, Portsmouth, Fulham (1920-1925)*. Joined from home-town club Worksop Town in 1911 and lived in the City until his death in 1948. He had become licensee of the Milton Arms after his playing days and it was there that he died. This was as a result of gas poisoning in 1948, he was only 53.

PROSINECKI, Robert

35 apps, 9 goals (2001-2002)
Career: *Dynamo Zagreb, Red Star Belgrade, Real Madrid, Oviedo, Barcelona, Sevilla, Croatia Zagreb, Hrvatski Dragovoljac, Standard Liege, Portsmouth, Olimpija Ljubljana, NK Zagreb (1986-2004)*. One season was all that was needed for the Croatian superstar to establish himself as one of the club's all time greats. His performances in midfield during the 2001/2 season were international class even though he was approaching the end of a glittering career. Having been the lynchpin in the side that had successfully avoided relegation he decided to return home to play for Olimpija Ljubljana. He is now assistant manager of the Croatian national team.

PULIS, Tony

(Manager between January and October 2000.)
Was temporary manager at Bristol City when Milan Mandaric persuaded him to take over at Pompey in January 2001. Results did not go his way and he was replaced ten months later by Steve Claridge. Has been in charge of Stoke City, for the second time, since June 2006.

PULLAR, David

105 apps, 7 goals (1975-1979)
Career: *Portsmouth, Exeter City, Crewe Alexandra (1975-1987)*. Pullar was a popular winger who successfully made the transition from the youth set up to first team regular. He played consistently through what was a fairly bleak period in the club's history and was sold to Exeter City following relegation to the Fourth Division. The Devon club broke their transfer record to secure his signature and their investment was rewarded with their new signing playing some of the best football of his career and being voted Player of the Year in his first season. His last club was Crewe Alexandra before he returned to Hampshire to run the Fountain Inn in Rowlands Castle. He has since worked as a parcel delivery driver and had a spell in on the Fratton Park staff, working in the Community Department.

PURDIE, Ian

5 apps, 1 goal (1979-1980)
Career: *Motherwell, Wigan Athletic,*
Portsmouth, Bangor City (1978-1979).
Former Scottish under 23 international scored
a vital goal during his short stay. Having
joined from Wigan in a £20,000 deal he found
the net in the last game of the 1979/80 season
which resulted in promotion from the Fourth
Division on goal difference. Now lives in
Glasgow.

QUASHIE, Nigel

163 apps, 14 goals (2000-2005)
Career: *Queens Park Rangers, Nottingham*
Forest, Portsmouth, Southampton, West
Bromwich Albion, West Ham United, Queens
Park Rangers (1995-date). Scottish
international Quashie joined Pompey in
August 2000 for £600,000 and was a regular
starter for five years. He followed Harry
Redknapp to Southampton for over £2 million
in 2005 and has played for numerous clubs
since, the most recent being QPR until his
release at the end of the 2009/10 season. His
name is still chanted at Fratton Park whenever
an opposing striker misses the goal by a
wide margin.

Photo: cultzeros

QUINN, Mick

137 apps, 68 goals (1985-1989)
Career: *Derby County, Wigan A, Stockport*
Co, Oldham Ath, Portsmouth, Newcastle U,
Coventry C, Plymouth A, Watford (1978-1995).
Micky Quinn used to joke that he was the
fastest player in the league over one yard. It is
true that he may not have been quick but he
certainly had any eye for goal. He hit the
target 68 times in five years for Pompey and
was top scorer when the team won promotion
to the First Division in 1987. During his
playing days he picked up a number of
nicknames including 'Sumo' due to his slightly
overweight (!) frame and the crowd chant of
'who ate all the pies?' was later used as the
title for his autobiography. Once retired from
football, Quinn became a race horse trainer
He now has stables at Newmarket, Suffolk and
can be heard on TalkSport radio commenting
on both sports. *Player of the season in 1989.*

RADCLIFFE, Vince

14 apps (1964-1967)
Career: *Portsmouth, Peterborough United,*
Rochdale (1964-1968). Centre half Radcliffe
first signed up as a fifteen year old in 1960
and was primarilly used as understudy to
Jimmy Dickinson. He made the bulk of his
appearances when Jim was rested but a
broken leg sustained in a match against
Southampton in 1964 meant a long period out
of the side and ultimately his release. Played
for Peterborough and won promotion from the
fourth division with Rochdale before retiring
in 1968. Emigrated to Australia in 1973 and
has been involved with the game 'down
under' ever since. Having played, coached
and managed, he then moved into an
administrative role with local club Inglewood
United, who are based in Perth.

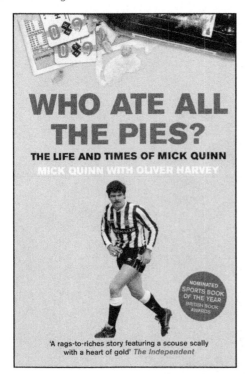

WHO ATE ALL THE PIES?

THE LIFE AND TIMES OF MICK QUINN

MICK QUINN WITH OLIVER HARVEY

NOMINATED
SPORTS BOOK
OF THE YEAR
BRITISH BOOK
AWARDS

'A rags-to-riches story featuring a scouse scally
with a heart of gold' *The Independent*

RADOSAVLJEVIC, Preki

45 apps, 7 goals (1994-1995)
Career: *Everton, San Jose, Portsmouth, Kansas City Wizards, Miami Fusion, Kansas City Wizards (1982-2005).* A broken arm sustained shortly after Jim Smith had brought the Yugoslavian from Everton meant that it took several months before 'Preki' could stamp his authority on the side. Once in the first XI, he produced some outstanding displays and it was disappointing to see him go at the end of his only season at the club. His visa had expired and this prompted a move across the water to America. He has since won the Most Valuable Player award twice and represented the United States in the 1998 World Cup. Having retired as a player he became a coach with Chivas USA and was named Coach of the Year in his first season in charge. Is now the head coach of Toronto FC in Major League Soccer.

RAFFERTY, Billy

98apps, 40 goals (1980-1983)
Career: *Coventry City, Blackpool, Plymouth Argyle, Carlisle United, Wolves, Newcastle United, Portsmouth, Bournemouth (1969-1985).* It was a fruitful striking partnership formed with Paul Mariner at third club Plymouth that kick-started Rafferty's career. He was 26 when he signed for Pompey in 1980 for a fee of £80,000 and the goals continued to flow. He was part of the Third Division championship winning side before moving to Bournemouth for £8,000 in 1983. His career came to a close in Portugal where he stayed for three years before opening his own health & fitness centre. More recently he has been organising six a side tournaments.

RAFFERTY, Ron

23 apps, 5 goals (1954-1957)
Career: *Wycombe Wanderers, Shrewsbury Town, Portsmouth, Grimsby Town, Hull City, Aldershot (1953-1968).* A popular striker who went onto become a goalscoring hero at Grimsby Town. First spotted playing for Wycombe, he found his path blocked by Derek Weddle and Syd McLellan and only managed the occasional outing during his three years on the club's books. Later returned south to become player/coach at Guildford City and was a sales representative with Lyons Cakes for 16 years. Hip problems forced to give up work at the age of 54 and he now lives in retirement in Addlestone, Surrey.

REAGAN, Martin

5 apps (1952-1953)
Career: *York City, Hull City, Middlesbrough, Shrewsbury Town, Portsmouth, Norwich City (1946-1955).* Already an experienced outside-left when Shrewsbury Town accepted Pompey's bid of £15,000 in 1952. As a player he failed to make much of an impact but went on to have a long and successful coaching career once he hung up his boots. He spent the summers in America, managed the England Ladies team for twelve years and continued to coach until he was 80.

Photo: www.playersincevents.co.uk

REDKNAPP, Harry

(Manager 2002-2004 and 2005-2008.)
Love him or hate him, there is no doubt that Harry Redknapp carved his name into the history of Portsmouth Football Club. Has been manager of Tottenham Hotspur since leaving the club for a second time in 2008.

REES, Derek

46 apps, 15 goals (1954-1957)
Career: *Portsmouth, Ipswich Town (1954-1960).* Goalscoring winger who joined from the Army in 1954. Died in Wales in May 1998.

REES, Jason

48 apps, 3 goals (1994-1996)
Career: *Luton Town, Mansfield Town (loan), Portsmouth, Exeter City (loan), Cambridge United, Exeter City. (1988-2000).* A free transfer from Luton who although a full Welsh international struggled to break into the first team and was was allowed to join Cambridge United. Rees now manages South West Peninsula League side Exeter Civil Service, having previously held a similar post at Ottery St Mary.

He had signed for Stockport County in 1936 but had to wait until 1946 for his big chance. This came in an £7,000 move to Pompey who, with his help, were to win the League in subsequent years - it was his hat-trick on the last day of the 1949/50 season that secured the title on goal difference. 'Thunderboots' continued to knock in the goals, 146 in total, one of which, a penalty, literally burst the net. Having won over an initially sceptical crowd, he became one of Pompey's greatest ever strikers and played up until the ripe old age of 38. After a short spell at non-league Tonbridge, Duggie returned to Fratton Park and worked as Head Groundsman until 1978. He then ran a youth hostel for the club before retiring to Widley, Portsmouth. Died in Park Gate in February 2002 (aged 84)

REID, Micky

5 apps, 1 goal (1950-1951)
Career: *Wolverhampton Wanderers, Bournemouth, Portsmouth, Watford (1947-1952).* Midlander who played mainly in the reserves following his free transfer from Bournemouth. Became a teacher and was at one time a senior lecturer at Highbury Technical College. Died in April 1975 at the age of 48. He was found in a garden in Compton Road North End.

REID, Duggie

329 apps, 136 goals (1946-1955)
Career: *Stockport County, Portsmouth, Tonbridge (1936-1956).* The Second World War delayed Duggie Reid's rise to prominence.

REILLY, Matt

138 apps (1899-1904)
Career: *Royal Artillery, Portsmouth, Dundee, Notts County, Tottenham Hotspur, Shelbourne (1893-1909).* An Irish international keeper who played for the club in the early 1900's. He was known "Gunner Reilly" and later became a publican in Southsea.He died in his native Dublin in December 1954, aged 80.

REYNOLDS, Richie

160 apps, 28 goals (1971-1976)
Career: *Plymouth Argyle, Portsmouth (1965-1976).* The former Plymouth hitman might never have played for Pompey had he not chosen the security of a two year contract instead of a shorter deal being offered by Manchester City. He put pen to paper in June 1971 and only took a week to bag his first goal for the club. He ended the season as top scorer and winner of the Player of the Year award. During his stay he was paired with a variety of striking partners but had to endure relegation and was finally released in 1976. Played in Holland and America before managing local teams Chichester City and Petersfield. Having always been a passionate race-goer, he set up a company selling shares in race horses. This has led to ownership of such fine names as: Fratton Park, Play Up Pompey, Star of Pompey, and even Blue Army.

RITCHIE, Paul

12 apps (2002-2003)
Career: *Heart of Midlothian, Bolton Wanderers (loan), Rangers, Manchester City, Portsmouth (loan), Derby County (loan), Walsall, Dundee United, AC Omonia, Carolina Railhawks (1992-2009).* Appeared in 12 games on loan from Manchester City in 2002/3 but was not offered a permanent deal despite being a Scottish international. Became assistant manager of US side Carolina Railhawks in April 2010.

RIX, Graham

(Manager between Feb 2001 and March 2002.)
Despite being an excellent player and successful coach, Rix was less successful as a manager. His year in charge at Pompey was terminated in March 2002 to make way for Harry Redknapp and a subsequent spell at Oxford United only lasted seven months. Served six months in prison for having underage sex with a minor, while assistant manager at Chelsea but returned to the club and was appointed caretaker boss when Vialli left. Is now a coach at the Glenn Hoddle Academy in Southern Spain.

ROBERT, Laurent

17 apps, 1 goal (2005-2006)
Career: *Montpellier, Paris Saint-Germain, Newcastle United, Portsmouth (loan), Benfica, Levante, Derby County, Toronto FC, Larissa. (1994-2009).* A brilliant player on his day, who possessed the ability to strike the ball with great accuracy particularly from free kicks. Capped by France, his career was marred by a series of disciplinary bust-ups. As a result of one of these, Newcastle United were keen to offload the unpredictable Frenchman and let him team up with the Blues on a long term loan. Unfortunately his temperament let him down again and at one time he stormed out of Fratton Park having refused to sit on the bench as a substitute. It was not long before he was sent back to Tyneside. Robert has since 'entertained' crowds and club management in Portugal, Spain and Canada. He also had a brief return to England with Derby County but his most recent employers were Cypriot side Larissa.

ROBERTS, Jason MBE

12 apps, 4 goals (2003-2004)
Career: *Hayes, Wolves,, Bristol Rovers, WBA Portsmouth (loan), Wigan A, Blackburn R (1995-date).* Grenadian striker who has been an established Premiership player for many years now and was awarded the MBE in the 2010 New Years Honours list for services to sport. In 2003/4 he played four games on loan at Fratton Park and scored his solitary Pompey goal against Everton. Has been with Blackburn Rovers since July 2006.

ROBERTS, Phil

179 apps, 1 goal (1973-1978)
Career: *Bristol Rovers, Portsmouth, Hereford United, Exeter City (1968-1982).* Welsh international full back whose four club career was spread across three decades. He had earned his call up to the national side following impressive displays in the heart of the Pompey defence. Was part of John Deacon's transformation of the club, having joined from Bristol Rovers for £55,000 in 1973 and then establishing himself as a robust and reliable defender. Became a self-employed builder in Whimple near Exeter, then moved to Bangkok, Thailand after setting up a bicycles export business.

Carl Robinson *Photo: Longbomb*

ROBERTS, Trevor

3 apps (1978-1980)
Career: *Portsmouth, Basingstoke Town (1978-1980).* A 6ft 4'' defender who was part of the squad that won promotion from the Fourth Division in 1979/80. Roberts is now partner in a property development business.

ROBINSON, Carl

20 apps (2002-2004)
Career: *Wolverhampton Wanderers, Portsmouth, Sunderland, Norwich City, Toronto FC, New York Red Bulls (1995-date).* Welsh international defender who joined the club on a 'Bosman' free transfer from Wolves in 2002 and was part of the team that won promotion that season. Won 52 caps with his country and played for Sunderland and Norwich before taking a paycut to move to play in Canada. Cheaper property prices meant that he was able to buy a country estate close to his new side, Toronto FC. He was voted the Canadian club's Most Valuable player for each of his first two seasons but is now playing for the New York Red Bulls in Major League Soccer.

ROBINSON, Matt

77 apps, 1 goal (1997-2000)
Career: *Southampton, Portsmouth, Reading, Oxford United, Forest Green Rovers, Salisbury City, Totton (1993-date).* Alan Ball returned to one of his former clubs, Southampton, to snap up Robinson for £15,000. The defender spent two seasons playing in the left back berth before new manager Tony Pulis sold him to Reading for £200,000 in 2000. Decided to train to become a Policeman and has played non-league soccer for Forest Green, Salisbury and since February 2009, AFC Totton.

ROCHFORD, Bill

43 apps, 1 goal (1938-1939)
Career: *Portsmouth, Southampton, Colchester United (1931-1951).* Rochford (known as 'Rocky') was a member of the 1939 FA Cup winning team. He played over 100 matches for Pompey and Southampton. Following his retirement, Rochford returned to his native north-east to become a farmer near Gateshead, but continued to scout for Southampton. He died at Bishop Auckland in March 1984.

Bill Rochford

RODIC, Aleksandar

4 apps (2004-2005)
Career: *NC Gorica, Portsmouth, Kayserispor, PFC Litex Lovech (1998-date).* Slovenian who joined the club on deadline day in January 2005, but could not break into the starting eleven and was loaned to Turkish club Kayserispor after only four appearances. Rodic was released in the summer of 2006 and signed by Bulgarian club Litex Lovech In February 2010 he signed for Chinese Super League club Qingdao Jonoon in a loan deal.

ROGERS, Alan

192 apps, 17 goals (1979-1984)
Career: *Plymouth Argyle, Portsmouth, Southend United, Cardiff City (1973-1986).* Devonian winger who had taken to the position while playing at school and continued to torment defenders from the flank for the whole of his career. At Plymouth Argyle he had played with future Pompey players Paul Mariner and Steve Davey before Frank Burrows signed him with some of the £150,000 the club had received from Steve Foster's transfer to Brighton. Over 150 games and two managers later, Alan was sold to Southend United where he played for the great Sir Bobby Moore. However, the club was suffering financially and he was released

to be re-united with Frank Burrows, who by this time was in charge at Cardiff City. With an eye to the future, Alan and his wife purchased the Swinton Guest House in Plymouth, which they have operated successfully ever since.

ROLLINGS, Andy

36 apps, 1 goal (1981-1983)
Career: *Norwich City, Brighton & H A, Swindon Town, Portsmouth, Cardiff City, Torquay United, Brentford, Aldershot, Brighton & HA (1973-1987).*
Bristol born Rollings started at Norwich but made his name at Brighton initially under Brian Clough and then alongside Steve Foster heart of Seagull's defence. Pompey signed him from Swindon Town for £5,000 towards end of career. He played a handful of games but when Bobby Campbell replaced Frank Burrows it seemed like a good time to leave. His wife had opened a tearoom in Brighton so he decided to hang up his boots and join her.

ROOKES, Phil

121 apps (1938-1951)
Career: *Worksop Town, Bradford City, Portsmouth, Colchester United, Chichester City (1937-1952).* Played for Pompey either side of the Second World War during which time he served on HMS Arganaut with the Royal Navy. A solid right-back, he captained the side on the day that Pompey reached the top of the First Division for the first time in their history. He was a member of the championship-winning teams of 1948–49 and 1949–50 before leaving to play for Colchester United. Retired to Norfolk and died in 2003.

ROSS, Trevor

5 apps (1982-1983)
Career: *Arsenal, Everton, Portsmouth (loan), AEK Athens, Sheffield United, Bury, Hyde United, Altrincham (1974-1988).* Scotland Under 21 former Arsenal and Everton right back. He played five games on loan from the Goodison Park club in 1982/3 but played out the rest of his career in Greece and the lower divisions of the league. After leaving football, Ross worked as an HGV driver. and then became a transport supervisor. Also coached youngsters at Oldham Sports Centre.

Photo: dalli58

ROUTLEDGE, Wayne

13 apps (2005-2006)
Career: *Crystal Palace, Tottenham Hotspur, Portsmouth (loan), Fulham (loan), Aston Villa, Cardiff City (loan), Queens Park Rangers, Newcastle United (2001-date).* England Under 21 midfielder with bags of talent but took a long time to consistently produce the results that his early form had promised. Now playing for Newcastle United.

ROWE, Tommy

46 apps (1938-1939)
Career: *Portsmouth (1938-1939).* Was the last surviving member of Pompey's 1939 cup winning side when he died in May 2006. During the war he served as a bomber pilot and won the Distinguished Flying Cross as well as being a Prisoner of War for 14 months. As a player, Rowe was a slender centre half with skill rather than brute force and served the club well. At the end of his career he settled in Poole until his death at the age of 92.

RUDONJA, Mladen

18 apps (2000-2002)
Career: *Sint-Truidinese VV, Portsmouth, NK Olimpija., Apollon Limassol, Anorthosis Famagusta, Koper, NK Olimpija (1991-2009).* A Slovenian striker who won 65 caps for his country and became a minor national hero nicknamed 'Turbo Rudi'. In spite of endless energy and determination he failed to make an impression during his 18 games for the club. Eventually returned to play for one of his former clubs, NK Olimpija Ljubljana with former Pompey teammate Robert Prosinecki.

RUSSELL, Kevin

5 apps (1985-1987)
Career: *Brighton, Portsmouth, Wrexham, Leicester City, Stoke City, Burnley, Bournemouth, Notts County, Wrexham (1982-2002).* Former youth player who went to enjoy a long career with ten different clubs. He is now working as an assistant manager for Preston North End.

RUSSELL, Lee

146 apps, 3 goals (1988-1996) Former YTS trainee whose eleven years as a pro at the club were hampered by a series of injuries. one of which kept him out of the FA Cup semi-final against Liverpool. A reliable left-back he only made just over 100 league games in over a decade. It was another knee injury that ultimately ended his playing days while on the books at Torquay United. He stayed in the area and trained to become an electrician. Now lives in Paignton and runs his own business in nearby Torquay.

RUTTER, Cyril

185 apps (1953-1962)
Career: *Portsmouth (1953-1962).* A tough centre half who had only switched from rugby to football after he left school. He was working as an apprentice at the dockyard when he was offered the chance to become a Pompey player. For the next decade he did his best to prevent the club's slide down the league and never gave less than 100%. Became director of coaching for the US Forces based in Germany and took over as player/manager of Salisbury City upon his return home. As well as running a bike shop in Southsea, at one time he owned a restaurant in Hayling Island with former team-mate Peter Harris. Cyril continued to play for the ex-Pros XI but is now retired and lives in Portsmouth.

RYDER, Terry

16 apps, 4 goals (1950-1952)
Career: *Norwich City, Portsmouth, Swindon Town (1946-1952).* Ryder had impressed for Norwich in cup games against Pompey and this prompted a £6,000 switch to the south coast. Only 5' 4'' tall he tried valiantly in each of his appearances but struggled to make the leap up from third to first division. Played for Swindon and in non-league soccer before a broken leg ended his career. Worked as a wire weaver and foreman in Norwich until his retirement.

SAHAR, Ben

0 apps (2008)
Career: *Chelsea, QPR (loan), Sheffield Wednesday (loan), Portsmouth (loan), De Graafschap (loan), Espanyol (2006-date).* Great things were expected from Israeli born Sahar. He agreed a six month loan from Chelsea, played in a number of pre-season games and was an unused sub in three league matches. However, he returned to Stamford Bridge without a single official appearance to his name. Sahar moved to Espanyol for a fee of £1million in the summer of 2009 but is now back in Israel playing for Hapoel Tel Aviv.

SANDFORD, Lee

89 apps, 2 goals (1985-1990)
Career: *Portsmouth, Stoke City, Sheffield United, Reading (loan), Stockport County (loan), Woking (1985-2003).* Former apprentice who first made the leap to first team action as seventeen year old and played intermittently over the next three seasons. When called upon, he always gave good service and even spent most of one game in goal after Alan Knight had been stretchered off. Alan Ball who by now was Stoke City boss returned to the club to pick up his former player for £140,000 in December 1989. Later moved to Sheffield United for £500,000 and also played for Reading and Stockport. During his career, he had always had a keen interest in stocks and shares and now teaches others how to make money on the stock market.

SAUNDERS, Ron

259 apps, 156 goals (1958-1964)
Career: *Everton, Tonbridge Angels, Gillingham, Portsmouth, Watford, Charlton Athletic (1951-1967).* One of the greatest strikers in the club's history, Saunders topped the goalscoring chart for six consecutive seasons. He could shoot equally effectively with either foot and by the time he left for Watford he had scored 156 goals in 259 appearances. Manager George Smith endured a fair amount of criticism when he made the decision to accept £15,000 for the goal machine in 1964. An equally impressive management career followed his on-pitch exploits. Having successfully managed a number of clubs, his highlight must have been leading Aston Villa to the First Division championship in 1980/1.

SCHEMMEL, Sebastien

18 apps, 1 goal (2003-2004)
Career: *Nancy, Metz, West Ham United, Portsmouth, Le Havre (1993-2005).* Schemmel had been a popular player at West Ham and had won their Player of the Year trophy in 2001/2. But a loss of form the following year saw him fall out of favour and ended with a move to the south coast. He made 12 appearances in blue but could not recapture his early success and returned home to France where he finished his career with Le Havre.

SCOULAR, Jimmy

268 apps (1946-1953)
Career: *Portsmouth, Newcastle United, Bradford Park Avenue (1945-1964).* Once described by Duncan Edwards as "the finest tackler of the ball that I have ever seen", Jimmy Scoular was born in Scotland but signed for Pompey from Gosport Borough. War-time naval service had brought him down to H.M.S. Dolphin and he had been playing for the Navy when first spotted. He played right-half throughout the glory years at the end of the forties/early fifties and won nine Scottish caps. Success followed him to Newcastle United, who he joined in 1953. At St James' Park he was made Captain and led his side to victory in the 1955 FA Cup final. In total he made over 600 League games before turning his hand to management. Was in charge at Cardiff City and Newport County before scouting for a number of clubs. Died in March 1998 at the age of 73.

SENIOR, Trevor

13 apps, 2 goals (1981-1982)
Career: *Dorchester Town, Portsmouth, Aldershot (loan), Reading, Watford, Middlesbrough, Reading, Woking, Dorchester Town, Farnborough Town (1981-1996).* Senior started his career at Dorchester where he played up front with Graham Roberts. He joined Pompey in 1981 for £35,000, but this proved to be little more than a career stepping stone. It was at his next club, Reading that he started to consistently find the back of the net. In his first season he bagged 36 goals and was the division's top scorer. Later managed Weymouth, Bridport and Bridgewater. Now lives in Dorchester and has been coaching in local schools for the past fifteen years.

Photo: Antonia Sterland

SHARPE, Lee

17 apps (2000-2001)
Career: *Torquay U, Man U, Leeds United, Sampdoria, Bradford City, Portsmouth (loan), Exeter City, (1988-2004).* Sharpe went from 17 year old trainee at Torquay to first team player at Manchester United. At Old Trafford he won a cabinet full of trophies including England caps at Under 23, 'B' and full level. He had also been the subject of a £4.5 million move to Leeds United, played in Italy for Sampdoria, and joined Bradford City by the time he signed for Pompey on loan in 2000. He is now a regular on out TV screens in a variety of programmes which have ranged from an appearance in Coronation Street to 'Celebrity Love Island'. In between takes, he is also an official after dinner speaker for Manchester United.

SHEARING, Peter

19 apps (1961-1963)
Career: *West Ham, Portsmouth, Exeter City, Plymouth Argyle, Bristol Rovers, Gillingham (1960-1973).* 6ft 1" keeper who was brought to the club to challenge Dick Beattie. When Beattie left the club the following year it looked as though Shearing would make the position his own but when John Armstrong was brought in and a young challenger called John Milkins appeared on the scene, his hopes receded. Played for Plymouth, Exeter and Gillingham until a broken arm ended his career. Is now retired having run a Post Office in Kent. Was also a Parish Councillor with a reputation for being able to do a mean Tommy Cooper impression.

SHERINGHAM, Teddy

38 apps, 10 goals (2003-2004)
Career: *Millwall, Nottingham Forest, Tottenham Hotspur, Manchester United, Tottenham Hotspur, Portsmouth, West Ham United, Colchester United (1983-2008).* Many pundits thought that Sheringham's career was drawing to a close when he signed for Pompey in 2003. It soon became apparent that he had the same fitness and stamina of players considerably younger than himself and he went on to play competitively until the age of 42. His contract at Fratton Park was only for one season but he played in most games and scored a creditable 10 goals. Upon release, he was not prepared to accept that he was finished and managed to play for West Ham for a further three years, winning the Championship Player of the Year award by scoring 20 of the goals that earned the Hammers a return to the Premiership. In 2006 at the age of 41, he broke his own record for being the Premiership's oldest scorer with a goal against... Pompey! (We won 2-1 though.) Retirement finally came at the end of the 2007/8 season having tried in vain to help Colchester United avoid relegation. His son Charlie is now following in dad's footsteps. He started as a junior at Millwall and Tottenham but is currently playing for Dartford Town..

SHERWOOD, Tim

33 apps, 3 goals (2002-2004)
Career: *Watford, Norwich City, Blackburn Rovers, Tottenham Hotspur, Portsmouth, Coventry City (1987-2005).* Joined Pompey from Tottenham Hotspur but he had previously led Blackburn Rovers to the 1993/4 Premiership title. Winner of three England caps, he had fallen out with Glenn Hoddle at Spurs and agreed to a loan period at Fratton Park. This was turned into a permanent move and he helped the club win the First Division in his first season. A broken leg sustained during the 2002/3 campaign kept him out of the side and he was released along with Teddy Sheringham when his contract expired. After a few games with Coventry, Sherwood conceded that his career was at an end and agreed to become part of Harry Redknapp's backroom staff at Tottenham Hotspur in October 2008.

SHOTTON, Malcolm

12 apps (1987-1988)
Career: *Leicester CIty, Nuneaton Borough, Oxford United, Portsmouth, Huddersfield Town, Barnsley, Hull City, Ayr United, Barnsley (1974-1996).* Only stayed six months following a move from Oxford United in 1987 before moving on to Huddersfield for £50,000 less than the original £70,000 paid to secure his signature. He had been a regular fixture in the Oxford side and later returned to the club as manager. Also served Bradford City as assistant manager but became Director of Football at Loughborough University in 2006.

SHOWERS, Derek

45 apps, 8 goals (1978-1981)
Career: *Cardiff City, Bournemouth, Portsmouth, Hereford United. (1970-1983).* Blond haired Welsh striker who was nicknamed 'Nookie Bear ' thanks to his likeness to Roger DeCourcey. Signed in a £13,000 deal from Bournemouth but had to recover from an early injury before forming a striking partnership with David Gregory. When the goals dried up he was dropped and then sold to Hereford United in November 1980. After leaving Hereford he had spells playing non-league football for Dorchester Town and Barry Town before retiring. He later became involved with the Cardiff City youth programme before going to work for the Royal Mail. Now lives in Merthyr Tydfil, works as a delivery driver and also helps compile statistics for the F.A.

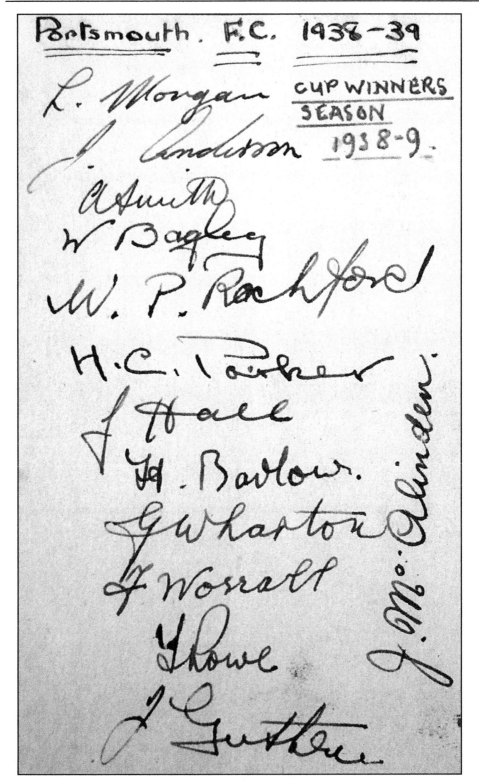

Portsmouth. F.C. 1938-39

CUP WINNERS
SEASON
1938-9.

R. Morgan
J. Anderson
A Smith
W Bagley
W. P. Rochford
H. C. Parker
J Hall
H. Barlow.
G Wharton
F Worrall
Howe
J Guthrie

J. Mc Alinden.

SILK, Gary
1 app (2003-2006)
Career: *Portsmouth, Barnet (loan), Notts County, Mansfield Town (2003-date).* Former youth player who made his League debut while on loan to Barnet. Having only made one appearance, the Isle of Wight born defender was released at the end of the 2005/6 season. He now plays for Mansfield Town where he has earned a reputation as one of the best right backs in the Conference and won the club Player of the Year award.

SILVA, Dario
15 apps, 3 goals (2005-2006)
Career: *Defensor Sporting, Penarol, Cagliari, Espanyol, Malaga CF, Sevilla, Portsmouth (1992-2006).* Uruguayan international striker who arrived at Fratton Park from Sevilla with a reputation as a "frenzied attacker". He certainly tried hard but an ankle injury contributed to his early release in February 2006 after only 15 matches. The following October he was involved in a car accident back home in Montevideo which resulted in the amputation of the lower part of one of his legs. He had lost control of his pick up truck and suffered a fractured skull and a compound fracture to his right leg. Remarkably, following several years of rehabilitation he returned to knock in a phenomenal 40 goals in 31 games for a local semi-professional side. An inspiration to fellow amputees, he has since run numerous marathons and even scored a penalty whilst playing in a charity game for a Uruguay XI against Argentina.

SIMPSON, Fitzroy
169 apps, 10 goals (1995-2000)
Career: *Swindon Town, Manchester City, Bristol City (loan), Portsmouth, Hearts, Walsall, Telford United, Linfield, Havant & Waterlooville, Eastleigh (1988-date).* In a twenty year career, the 169 games played for Pompey were the most that Fitzroy Simpson made for any one club and were arguably his best days. During his stay he represented Jamaica at the 1998 World Cup finals and was a regular fixture until his move to Hearts in 2000. After a spell on the Costa Del Sol working in property he returned to the south five years later and turned out for both Havant and Eastleigh. Simpson has since worked as a fitness coach and set up a company that supplies luxury cars to among other people, successful footballers.

SKOPELITIS, Giannis
18 apps (2004-2006)
Career: *Egaleo, Portsmouth, Egaleo, Atromitos, Anorthosis Famagusta (2005-date).* Skopelitis was brought to the club to replace the departing Amdy Faye on a year-long loan deal. Already a Greek international, he returned to Egaleo when the agreement expired. He now plays in Cyprus for Anorthosis Famagusta.

SMERTIN, Alexey
33 apps (2003-2004)
Career: *Chelsea, Portsmouth (loan), Charlton Athletic (loan), Dynamo Moscow, Fulham (1992-2008).* Winner of 55 Russian caps, Smertin came to Pompey in 2003 on loan from Chelsea. The London club had only just paid Bordeaux £3.45 million but felt that he would benefit from some first team experience elsewhere. After some impressive performances at Fratton Park, most notably in Pompey's 1–0 victory over Manchester United, Smertin returned to London New boss Jose Mourinho gave him a run in the team for the first third of the season but then reduced him to a bit part player and in January 2006 he was sold to Dynamo Moscow for £1 million. After his release from Fulham and failing to find a new club he went into politics in his native Russia and in March 2009 was elected as an MP for the Altai region of Russia.

Jack Smith

SMITH, Fred

96 apps, 1 goal (1970-1973)
Career: *Burnley, Portsmouth, Dallas Tornado, Halifax Town (1963-1975).* Smith joined the club in a joint deal with Burnley team-mate Colin Blant and made the right back spot his own for the the next two years. A cartilage injury ended his Pompey playing days and he spent 1973–74 in the United States with Dallas Tornado before ending his career with a season at Halifax Town. Was employed as a community worker by the Borough Council in Burnley, having previously had a milkround, restaurant and then a newsagents.

SMITH, George

72 apps, 3 goals (1967-1969)
Career: *Newcastle United, Barrow, Portsmouth, Middlesbrough, Birmingham City, Cardiff City, Swansea City, Hartlepool United (1963-1980).* Smith covered some miles during his eight club career with Portsmouth being his most southerly stop. Ended his career at Hartlepool and went into coaching. Now living in the north east where he set up his own academy which has discovered a number of current professionals including Michael Brown.

SMITH, George

(Manager between 1961 and 1970.)
A former Sergeant-Major who instilled a strict regime during his nine years as boss. He will also be remembered for doing away with the Reserve and Youth teams. Retired to live in Bodmin, Cornwall and died there in November 1983 aged 68.

SMITH, Jack

261 apps, 61 goals (1927-1934)
Career: *North Shields, Portsmouth, Bournemouth, Clapton Orient (1919-1936).* Scored twice on his debut following a £5 transfer from South Shields in 1927. He also scored the winning goal in the 1929 FA Cup semi-final against Aston Villa and won his first England cap at the age of 31, again scoring in his first game. He added two more caps and two more goals to his international tally. Moved to Bournemouth in 1934 and ended his playing days at Clapton Orient in 1936. Smith died in January 1977 at the age of 79

Photo: TwentiethApril1986

SMITH, Jim

(Manager between June 1991 and February 1995.) The 'Bald Eagle' came so close to success in his years as boss. An FA Cup semi final in 1992 against Liverpool was only lost on penalties, promotion to the First Division was missed on goal difference and the following year the same target was tantalisingly close before a play-off defeat ended the dream. He returned in 2002 as Harry Redknapp's assistant and he finally enjoyed promotion in their first year. Smith returned to the game in 2006 after a short gap, to re-join Oxford United as manager and Director. He relinquished his managerial duties in November 2007.

SNOWDON, Brian

129 apps (1959-1963)
Career: *Blackpool, Portsmouth, Millwall, Detroit, Margate, Crystal Palace (1955-1968).* A solid centre half who was originally set for a career in the police force until he caught the eye of League scouts. Spent four years at Fratton Park and was part of the squad that won the third division championship in 1961/2. Later turned out for Millwall, Detroit Cougars in America and Crystal Palace. Died in 1995 aged 60.

SOLEY, Steve

12 apps (1998-1999)
Career: *Portsmouth, Macclesfield Town, Carlisle United, Southport (1998-2002).* Signed from non-league Leek Town for £30,000 in 1998 but failed to break into the first team and was loaned out to Macclesfield Town. He was a proficient midfielder in the lower divisions and went on to give great service to a succession of clubs including Southport and Dagenham, playing well into his thirties.

SONGO'O, Franck

4 apps (2005-2008)
Career: *Portsmouth, Bournemouth (loan), Preston North End (loan), Crystal Palace (loan), Sheffield Wednesday (loan), Zaragoza, Real Sociedad (2005-date).* A Cameroonian international winger who signed for £250,000 in 2005 but only made four appearances over the best part of three years. He joined Real Sociedad in Spain in 2008.

SPENCE, Bill

19 apps (1949-1951)
Career: *Portsmouth, Queens Park Rangers (1949-1953).* Bill was offered a contract in 1947 following a successful trial and made his debut against Manchester United almost immediately. He was used largely as a stand in centre half to cover for injuries and was allowed to join second Division QPR in1951. He died in March 1993 aged 67.

SRNICEK, Pavel

4 apps (2003-2004)
Career: *Banik Ostrava, Newcastle United, Sheffield Wednesday, Brescia, AS Cosenza, Portsmouth, West Ham United, Beira-Mar, Newcastle United (1990-2007).* Has the honour of being the only keeper to receive 10 out of 10 rating in the Sun in a ten year period. The Czech international played three games on loan in 2003/4 but is best remembered for his time at Newcastle United. He was voted one of their most popular players of all time and fittingly ended his career in England at the end of a second spell at the same club and then returned to the Czech Republic to set up the Srnicek school of goalkeeping.

St John, Ian

(Manager between September 1974 and May 1977.) As a player the Saint could do no wrong - he was part of the Liverpool team for over a decade and a hero on Merseyside. However, his managerial career was a different matter. It started at former club Motherwell and then included a three year stay at Fratton Park. Although he managed to introduce a promising bunch of youngsters to the first team, results were patchy at best. Spells as assistant manager at Sheffield Wednesday and Coventry preceded a successful TV career as half of Saint & Greavsie. Now a popular after dinner speaker hosts his own radio show on Radio City 96.7.

STANDEN, Jim

13 apps (1970-1972)
Career: *Arsenal, Luton Town, West Ham United, Millwall, Portsmouth (1953-1972).* The mid-sixties proved to incredibly good for Standen who was a talented cricketer as well as a First Division goalie. He won a County Championship medal with Worcestershire and an FA Cup winners medal with West Ham in 1964. A Cup Winners' Cup medal was added the following year. He joined Pompey in 1970 to provide cover for John Milkins and was called upon 13 times before emigrating to America. The former stopper is now retired and lives in Fresno, California.

Gary Stanley

STANLEY, Gary

56 apps, 4 goals (1983-1986)
Career: *Chelsea, Fort Lauderdale, Everton, Swansea City, Portsmouth, Wichita Wings, Bristol City, Waterlooville (1971-1989).* Midfielder who played for three top level clubs before his time at Pompey. He started at Chelsea, moved to Everton for £350,000 and then played for Swansea City, who were enjoying the best spell in their history. When the Welsh club were relegated from the First Division, Stanley was released on a free transfer and snapped up by Bobby Campbell. He initially slotted into the midfield but was later employed successfully as a right back. Left the club in 1986 and played in the US for Wichita Wings before coming back to play for Bristol Rovers and Waterlooville. Now lives in the Portsmouth area, where he worked for a cable television company before becoming a sales rep for a firm called Colorama Pharmaceuticals.

STEFANOVIC, Dejan

125 apps, 3 goals (2003-2006)
Career: *Red Star Belgrade, Sheffield Wednesday, Perugia, OFK Belgrade, Vitesse Arnhem, Portsmouth, Fulham, Norwich City (1993-2009).* A cultured defender who hailed from Serbia and has worn the colours of the national side on 20 occasions. He had already experienced English football with Sheffield Wednesday but joined Pompey from Vitesse Arnhem in Holland for £1.85 million. Recruited to provide extra strength to the rear guard for the first season back in the Premiership, he was a popular addition and won the player of the Year award in 2005. Stefanovic retired in 2009 after short stays at Fulham and Norwich but surprised the football world by coming out of retirement to play for Havant & Waterlooville in October 2010.

STENHOUSE, Alex

5 apps, 1 goal (1956-1958)
Career: *Dundee United, Portsmouth, Southend United (1956-1960).* Former Scottish schoolboy international was serving his National Service at Aldershot when his Colonel who was a Pompey fan recommended him to the club. He played a handful of games before Freddie Cox took over from Eddie Lever as manager and sold him to Southend United. Later opened a newsagent's business in Southend and ran the Shrimpers club at Southend United until he retired.

Jimmy Stephen

STEPHEN, Jimmy

105 apps (1949-1955)
Career: *Bradford Park Avenue, Portsmouth, Yeovil. (1939-1955).* Pompey broke their transfer record by paying £15,000 to add Jimmy Stephen to their ranks. He was in the R.A.F. at the time but Bradford Park Avenue held his registration and demanded a fee for his release. As a full-back, he had earned international honours with Scotland and was part of the team that won the 1949-50 League title. Ike Clarke later persuaded Stephen to join him at Yeovil Town and he stayed in the west country to become player-coach at Bridgewater Town. When he moved back to Portsmouth the Scotsman worked for GEC as a wireman for five years and then for local timber companies until taking retirement.

STEPHENSON, Alan

106 apps, 1 goal (1972-1975)
Career: *Crystal Palace, West Ham, Fulham, Portsmouth, (1951-1974).* Pompey were Stephenson's first club outside the capital. He had previously played for Crystal Palace and West Ham before Ron Tindall organised his £32,000 transfer from the Hammers. Was a consistent performer for three seasons but was one of seven players released by Ian St John in 1975. Moved over to South Africa to play for Durban and his opponents in his first match included another old Pompey favourite, Albie McCann. Upon his return, Stephenson became youth coach at Leyton Orient and ran a pub in the area before becoming a Family Welfare Officer for Essex County Council. Now retired following a hip operation.

STEVENS, Gary

59 apps, 3 goals (1990-1992)
Career: *Brighton & H A, Tottenham Hotspur, Portsmouth (1979-1992).* 7 England caps. Former England international who was forced to quit the game due to injury after only a year with Pompey. Although born in Hillingdon, his first club had been Brighton & Hove Albion, where he starred in an FA Cup run and attracted the interest of Spurs, who took him back to north London for £350,000 in 1983. The defender come midfielder spent six years at White Hart Lane and won seven England caps. Frank Burrows initially signed him on loan in January 1990 but made the move permanent after a series of impressive displays. He injured one of his knees in a match against Plymouth in March 19991 and despite an artificial cruciate ligament being inserted, he never fully recovered and had to quit the game. After a short time as manager of Petersfield United, Stevens became sales director of a firm selling coolpacks and heatpacks. Latterly he been a regular presenter on television and radio for Sky and Talksport. Is currently Tony Adams's assistant at Gabala FC in Azerbaijan

STEWART, Ian

2 apps (1987-1988)
Career: *Queens Park Rangers, Millwall (loan), Newcastle United, Portsmouth, Brentford, Aldershot, Colchester United, Harrow Borough (1980-1993).* Won 31 caps with Northern Ireland while at his first club, Queens Park Rangers and was a member of their 1986 World Cup squad. Ian St John added him to his newly promoted team from Newcastle United on a free transfer in 1987 but he failed to shine. Only made two appearances and only one of those in the league. Later played for Aldershot and Colchester. He now works for the Irish Football Association.

STIMSON, Mark

77 apps, 4 goals (1992-1996)
Career: *Tottenham Hotspur, Newcastle United, Portsmouth, Southend United, Leyton Orient, Canvey Island, Grays Athletic (1985-2004).* Another acquisition from Newcastle United, who found himself surplus to requirements when the Geordies signed John Beresford from Pompey for £700,000. He was brought in on loan but Jim Smith saw enough to pay £100,000 for his signature. Very much a squad player, he appeared in the first team over the next three years before being allowed to join Southend United for £25,000. Leyton Orient were his last club before dropping down to non-league football with Canvey Island. He won one cap with the England Semi-Professional side before moving into management with Grays Athletic, Stevenage Borough and Gillingham. He has been in charge at Barnet since June 2010.

STOKES, Bobby

29 apps, 3 goals (1977-1978)
Career: *Southampton, Portsmouth, (1968-1980).*
Stokes shot to fame after scoring the winner in the 1976 FA Cup final for Southampton against Manchester United. He spent eight years at the Dell before joining Pompey in 1977. After football he worked at the Harbour View cafe in Southsea until his death in May 1995. He had contracted pneumonia and passed away at the age of 44. One of the suites at the St Mary's Stadium is named in his honour, as is one of the blocks of flats that have been built on the site of the old Dell.

STONE, Steve

80 apps, 10 goals (2002-2005)
Career: *Nottingham Forest, Aston Villa, Portsmouth, Leeds United (1989-2006).*
Having suffered two broken legs at a youngster at Nottingham Forest it is remarkable that Stone had a football career at all. Having missed a whole season, he recovered enough to earn a £5.5 million move to Aston Villa in 1999. When his manager John Gregory was fired and replaced by Graham Taylor he agreed to move to Pompey and immediately became an influential member of the team that won promotion to the Premiership. His three year deal expired in 2005 and new boss Alain Perrin allowed him to join Leeds United. He has since returned to his native north-east where he became a commentator for BBC Radio 5Live before joining the coaching staff at Newcastle United. In July 2010 he was promoted to reserve team assistant.manager .

STORRIE, Jim

49 apps, 13 goals (1969-1972)
Career: *Airdrieonians, Leeds United, Aberdeen, Rotherham United, Portsmouth, Aldershot, St Mirren, Waterlooville (1962-1971).* Scotsman who was first introduced to the league by Don Revie who had paid Airdrie £20,000 to bring him to Leeds United. It was another five seasons before he found himself at Fratton Park, having previously moved from Elland Road to Rotherham after 125 appearances. The £5,000 that George Smith had paid was instantly rewarded when Storrie took only a week to get his name on the scoresheet. He scored ten goals in his first season but when Ron Tindall took over in 1970, his first team chances diminished. Two years later he left the club to play for St Mirren in Scotland but was soon back south as a Waterlooville player and then manager. Has since managed St Johnstone, coached in Kuwait and worked in the Tryst Sports Centre in Lanarkshire. His last post before retiring to Kilsyth was working as a steward and porter at Stirling University.

STRANGE, Alfred

24 apps, 16 goals (1922-1924)
Career: *Portsmouth, Port Vale, Sheffield Wednesday, Bradford Park Avenue (1922-1936).* An England international who won 20 full caps. After retiring from football, he settled in his home town of Ripley in Derbyshire and worked as a poultry farmer. He died in October 1978 but the following year a room at the Ripley Leisure Centre was named the "Alf Strange Room" in his honour.

STRONG, Jim

62 apps (1934-1937)
Career: *Hartlepool , Chesterfield, Portsmouth, Gillingham, Walsall, Burnley (1933-1952).* Goalkeeper who joined for £2,000 as an 18 year old and went on to play 62 matches in the 1930's. The war effectively split his career into two halves, the latter portion being spent with Burnley where he made over 250 appearances. Strong remained in the area and ran a poultry farm until his death in 1989.

STYLES, Archie

28 apps (1979-1980)
Career: *Everton, Birmingham City, Peterborough United, Portsmouth (1967-1980).* Liverpool born left back who had been part of a British record transfer when he joined Birmingham City from Everton as part of the £350,000 deal that took Bob Latchford to Everton. Signed for Pompey in 1979 but after a good run an achilles tendon injury kept him out of the side. His place given to emerging youngster Keith Viney and was eventually forced to retire. He then became youth coach at Fratton Park. before returning to the midlands to live in Cradley.

Colin Sullivan

SUGRUE, Paul

4 apps (1984-1986)
Career: *Manchester City, Cardiff City, Middlesbrough, Portsmouth, Northampton Town, Newport County, Bridgend Town, Elo Kuopio (1980-1989).* Big Malcolm Allison first spotted Sugrue playing for non-league Nuneaton and paid £20,000 to take him to Manchester City in 1977. This was to be just one of his many clubs and he added Pompey to the list in 1984. Alan Ball secured his services on a free transfer but he only made two league appearances in 15 months. Having returned from a spell in Finland, the well travelled midfielder managed Nuneaton Borough and then became vice-chairman and manager of Merthyr Tydfil. He resigned in 2007 and most recently was reported to have been working as a First Aid trainer with former Welsh international Mark Aizlewood.

SULLIVAN, Colin

104 apps (1981-1984)
Career: *Plymouth Argyle, Norwich City, Cardiff City, Hereford United, Portsmouth, Swansea City, Locks Heath (1968-1986).* Having been born in Cornwall, the nearest league club to home was Plymouth Argyle and it was there that Sullivan made his debut at the age of 16. In doing so, he became the youngest player in their history. Ironically, the record had previously been held by Richie Reynolds. At Home Park he established himself as an accomplished left-back and won call ups to the England youth and Under-23 sides. After 230 appearances for the club he joined Norwich City for £70,000 in 1974. He became a first team regular for the next four years and helped the Norfolk side to promotion from the second division and to the League Cup final in 1975. With his career seemingly coming to an end, Pompey offered him a contract at the age of 31 and he seized the opportunity. He played in all of the remaining games in his first season and was an ever present in the third division championship winning side of 1982//3. Having settled in the area, he played for Locks Heath after a short spell at Swansea and became a postman. In between rounds of golf, the Cornishman has been running his own landscaping business since the early 1990's.

SUMMERBELL, Mark

5 apps (2001-2002)
Career: *Middlesbrough, Cork City (loan), Bristol City (loan), Portsmouth (loan), Carlisle United (1995-2004).* A midfielder borrowed from Middlesbrough in 2001/2. Last seen playing for South Moor Sports having previously appeared in the Wensleydale Creamery League for Redmire United. Now believed to be a postman in Durham.

SVENSSON, Mathias

51 apps, 12 goals (1996-1998)
Career: *IF Elfsborg, Portsmouth, Tirol Innsbruck, Crystal Palace, Charlton Athletic, Derby County (loan), Norwich City, IF Elfsborg (1996-2008).* Swedish striker who first caught the eye with IF Elfsborg, where he scored 15 goals in only 22 games. This prompted a £75,000 move to Fratton Park where he made a dramatic start. In his first full match he scored two goals, made another, was sent off and carried off the field on a stretcher. The remainder of his stay was less eventful and he was sold to Austrian side Innsbruck for £100,000 in 1998.

He did return to England to play for Crystal Palace (under Terry Venables and Terry Fenwick), Charlton Athletic, Derby County and Norwich City. The Swedish international then returned home to re-join his first club IF Elfsborg . He has was forced to retire in 2008 and is now their assistant manager

SWAIN, Kenny

128 apps (1985-1988)
Career: *Chelsea, Aston Villa, Nottingham Forest, Portsmouth, West Bromwich Albion (loan), Crewe Alexandra (1973-1992).* Swain had played for Chelsea and won the league championship and European Cup with Aston Villa before joining Pompey in 1983. He played in every game during the 1986/7 promotion year and was an almost ever present for the first year back in the top flight. Swain later went into management with Grimsby Town and Wigan Athletic. Between 2002 and 2004, Swain was Director of Football at Thomas Telford School and scouted for a number of clubs. He is now an FA coach working with the national under-16's and under 17's

Scott Symon

Mick Tait being inducted into the Hall of Fame

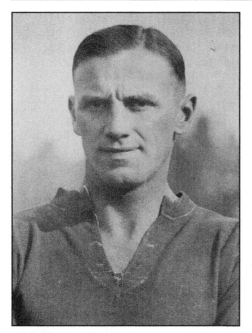

SYMON, Scott.

66 apps, 6 goals (1935-1938)
Career: *Dundee, Portsmouth, Rangers (1930-1947)*. Scotsman who ventured south of the border to spend three seasons at Fratton Park in the 1930's. He won one Scotland cap but went on to achieve success as a manager. He won the Scottish League Cup with his first club East Fife and was in charge when Preston North End reached the FA Cup final in 1953. As manager of his former club Rangers, he won six league championships and took them into Europe for the first time. Died in April 1985 (aged 73)

SYMONS, Kit

204 apps, 11 goals (1988-1995)
Career: *Portsmouth, Manchester City, Fulham, Crystal Palace (1988-2005)*.
Chistopher Jeremiah Symons is better known to us as 'Kit' and was the rock of the Pompey defence for seven years. During his Fratton Park days he was a fans' favourite, was the only Pompey player to score in the fateful FA Cup Semi Final penalty shoot out and was Player of the Year in 1994. A product of the youth set up, he created a formidable partnership with Andy Awford which led to speculation that one or both would be lured away by one of the nation's top sides. Symons did eventually move to Man City for £1.2 m to be reunited with former boss Alan Ball.

Later played for Crystal Palace and was briefly their caretaker manager before leaving the club in October 2007. Kit then joined Colchester United and again assumed the role of Caretaker Manager
Player of the season in 1994.

TAIT, Mick

282 apps, 33 goals (1980-1987)
Career: *Oxford United, Carlisle United, Hull City, Portsmouth, Reading, Darlington, Hartlepool United, Gretna, Hartlepool United (1974-1998)*. Geordie boy Tait served his league apprenticeship with Oxford, Carlisle and Hull but was still only 23 when Frank Burrows paid Hull City £100,000 for his signature. During the next seven years he gave sterling service but shifted position from attacker to midfield and finally to central defence. His battling performances won the crowd over and earned him a well deserved place in the club's Hall of Fame. Apart from a time with Reading, 'Yosser' has spent the years since in the north-east. He has had spells in management at Hartlepool and Darlington where he was also youth development officer. In May 2009, he was appointed manager of Blyth Spartans for a second time.

TARDIF, Chris

6 apps (2000-2002)
Career: *Portsmouth, Oxford United. (1998-2007).* Made his league debut in January 2001 after Russell Hoult was sold to West Brom and Aaron Flahavon was ruled out through injury. Stayed with the club until May 2004 but his opportunities were severely limited and he eventually joined Oxford United. Still lives in the area and has since played for Basingstoke Town Bognor Regis and his current club, Maidenhead United.

Photo: www.playersincevents.co.uk

TAVLARIDIS, Efstathios

5 apps (2002-2003)
Career: *Arsenal, Portsmouth (loan), Lille, Saint-Etienne (1997-date).* Greek defender who signed for Arsenal as a 21 year old. He was unable to displace Sol Campbell and Kolo Touré, and loaned to Pompey in 2002/3, making five appearances. In early 2004 he joined Lille OSC on a temporary basis and the deal was made permanent that summer. In June 2007, he signed a three year deal with Saint-Étienne

TAYLOR, Matt

203 apps, 29 goals (2002-2008)
Career: *Luton Town, Portsmouth, Bolton Wanderers (1999-date).* Matty's career started at Luton Town, having being rejected by home town club Oxford United, because they thought he was too fat. Pompey snapped him up in July 2002 for £750,000. The fee had been set by tribunal and left Luton boss Joe Kinnear seething. He was quoted as saying "at least Dick Turpin had the decency to wear a mask". Taylor provided a much needed spark as an attacking left sided midfielder but also had the knack of scoring sensational long range goals. The arrival of Niko Kranjčar in the 2007–08 season meant that Taylor was no longer assured a place in the starting XI and was sold to Bolton Wanderers in January 2008 for a fee believed to be in the region of £4 million.

TAYLOR, Tony

17 apps (1977-1978)
Career: *Morton, Crystal Palace, Southend United, Swindon Town, Bristol Rovers, Portsmouth, Kilmarnock, Albion Rovers, Northampton Town (1967-1980).* Taylor had already played left back for seven clubs before joining Pompey in February 1978. He managed to add 17 appearances to his tally before setting off on his travels again. He has since had stints in Canada, Greece, and a spell as assistant coach at Celtic in his Scottish homeland. He became coach of Canada's national boy's youth team in the 1980s and managed the national team during an unsuccessful bid to qualify for the 1990 FIFA World Cup finals. Now working as Technical Director of the Burlington Youth Soccer Club in Burlington, Ontario.

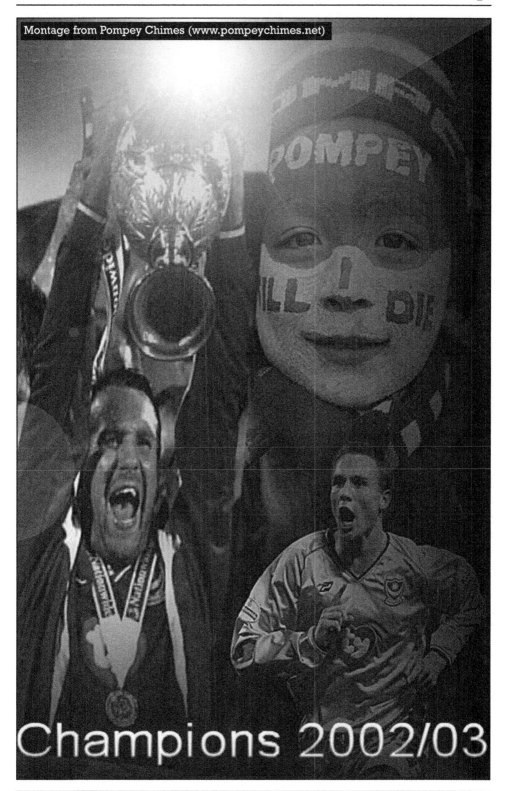

Montage from Pompey Chimes (www.pompeychimes.net)

Champions 2002/03

David Thackery

THACKERY, David

307 apps, 9 goals (1928-1936)
Career: *Motherwell, Portsmouth.* Played over 300 games including the 1929 and 1934 FA Cup Finals before a knee injury forced his retirement. He later worked for the Portsmouth and Gosport Gas Co and returned to Fratton Park as assistant groundsman. Dave died on 21st July 1954.

THOGERSEN, Thomas

115 apps, 8 goals (1998-2001)
Career: *BK Frem, Brondby IF, Portsmouth, BK Frem (1988-2002).* Thogerson had already won three Danish football championships with Brøndby IF before Alan Ball brought him to Fratton Park in a £100,000 deal. Initially used as a right back, he later flourished as an attacking midfielder and played over 100 games before returning to end his career with childhood club Frem.

THOMAS, Dave

35 apps (1982-1984)
Career: *Burnley, Queens Park Rangers, Everton, Wolves, Vancouver Whitecaps, Middlesbrough, Portsmouth (1966-1984).* Born in Kirkby-in-Ashfield, Dave came from good footballing stock - his grandfather was one of a group of West Auckland miners who represented Great Britain and won an international tournament held in Turin in the early 1910's. A former England international who was an extremely skillful and fast midfielder, he had a long and successful playing career, playing for almost 20 years and totalling over 450 league appearances whilst playing for Burnley, QPR, Everton, Vancouver Whitecaps, Middlesbrough, Pompey and Wolves (who he joined in preference to Manchester United, a decision that he has regretted ever since). He won 8 England caps overall whilst at QPR. In 1981, he played a single summer season with the Vancouver Whitecaps in the North American Soccer League. A three year spell at Pompey, towards the end of his career, was ended in 1986 by the new Deacon regime and he turned to one of his other passions, gardening, to earn a living for many years thereafter. He also worked part time as a PE teacher at the Bishop Luffa School in Chichester, but has now retired.

THOMAS, Jerome

3 apps (2008-2009)
Career: *Arsenal, Charlton Athletic, Portsmouth, West Bromwich Albion (2001-date).* A spine injury meant that former Arsenal youngster Thomas only made three appearances following his move from Charlton in 2008. He moved to current club, West Bromwich Albion the following year, in August 2009, on a free transfer. He was once mentioned in a rap song - London Town by Kano.

Photo: The Reeds and torkst

THOMAS, Michael

3 apps (1986-1987)
Career: *Arsenal, Portsmouth (loan), Liverpool, Middlesbrough (loan), Benfica, Wimbledon (1984-2001).* He is best remembered for scoring a last minute goal in injury time during the final match of the 1988-89 season which allowed Arsenal to claim the First Division title just ahead of Liverpool. Thomas spent a month on loan at Fratton Park before becoming a Liverpool player himself. He scored a goal for the Reds in the 1992 FA Cup Final and had spells at Benfica and Wimbledon before retiring in 2001. Now lives in Liverpool and runs his own security service. He also plays for the Liverpool masters team.

THOMAS, Rees

30 apps 0 goals (1959-1960)
Career: *Cardiff City, Torquay United, Brighton, Bournemouth, Portsmouth, Aldershot. (1950-1963)* Welshman who added Pompey to his list of clubs when he played 30 games at right back and helped the club retain their Second Division status when relegation looked more likely. Was released when George Smith took over and played for Aldershot before taking a job in the area as a lorry driver for World Books. Later ran a Post Office until problems with his spine forced an early retirement and a return to Wales.

THOMPSON, Bill

43 apps, 2 goals (1948-1953)
Career: *Carnoustie Panmure, Portsmouth, Bournemouth & B A (1948-1954).* Thompson played for Scottish junior club Carnoustie Panmure before joining Pompey's championship-winning teams of 1949 and 1950. He managed Worcester City and Exeter City and eventually returned to Fratton Park as caretaker after Freddie Cox's departure. Although he was not offered the job permanently he did work as George Smith's assistant before coaching in Holland Egypt. Lived in Portsmouth until his death on Boxing Day 1988.

THOMPSON, David

15 apps (2006-2007)
Career: *Liverpool, Swindon Town (loan), Coventry City, Blackburn Rovers, Wigan Athletic, Portsmouth, Bolton Wanderers (1996-2007).* Signed for Pompey in July 2006 on a one year deal, but was unhappy that he was not getting enough first team action and was sold to Bolton Wanderers just two hours before the transfer window shut on January 31, 2007 The following November he was forced to retire from the game at the age of 30 due to a chronic cartilage problem in his knee.

THOMSON, Andy

105 apps, 3 goals (1995-1999)
Career: *Swindon Town, Portsmouth, Bristol Rovers, Wycombe Wanderers, Forest Green Rovers. (1993-2006).* Thomson joined Pompey from his home town club Swindon for a fee of £75,000 in 1995 and played over 100 games before the club's financial problems forced his sale to Bristol Rovers for £50,000 in 1999. He became club captain at Rovers and also played for Wycombe Wanderers and Forest Green Rovers before retiring.

THORP, Hamilton

9 apps, 1 goal (1997-1998)
Career: *West Adelaide, Portsmouth (1996-1998).* Australian striker who measured 6ft 3" and scored one goal during his stay in 1997. After more than 16 years travelling the world, playing for 10 different clubs he has now settled back in Australia living in Bondi.

TILER, Carl

20 apps, 1 goal (2000-2003)
Career: *Barnsley, Notts F Swindon T , Aston Villa, Sheffield United, Everton, Charlton Athletic, Birmingham City (loan), Portsmouth (1988-2003).* A tough central defender who played for England Under 21s was signed by Graham Rix in 2001 for £250,000. He stayed for a couple of seasons, scoring once in the league against Crystal Palace, before finally retiring from the game in 2003 due to injury.

TILSED, Ron

15 apps (1972-1974)
Career: *Bournemouth & B A, Chesterfield, Arsenal, Portsmouth, Hereford United (1969-1974).* Weymouth born keeper who won England youth honours and played for Bournemouth, Chesterfield and Arsenal before joining Pompey, initially on loan, in 1973. A broken arm kept him out for most of his first season and David Best's arrival in February 1974 signalled the end to his short Pompey career. A free transfer took him to Hereford but he later moved over to Australia to play semi-professionally for Canberra City. Has been coaching goalkeepers 'down under' for many years now. Now involved in goalkeeper training with the Sutherland Sharks in the New South Wales Premier League. He still comes home to Poole in Dorset each year and catches up with his life long friend Kevin Bond.

TINDALL, Ron

181 apps, 9 goals (1964-1970)
Career: *Chelsea, West Ham United, Reading, Portsmouth (1952-1969).* Tindall was a London born centre forward who played at the highest level for Chelsea and West Ham, as well as proving to be a talented County level cricketer. He joined Pompey at a point where he was planning to retire from the game. However, an inspired switch of position, to defence, meant that he continued to play successfully for another five years. It also gave his first taste of coaching and management. By the time he finally left the club he had played all over the field (including ten minutes in goal), been captain, coach and had two spells as manager. He later emigrated to Perth in Australia, became their State Director of Sport and won the Western Australia Citizen of the Year for Sport.

Ron Tindall

TINN, Jack

(Manager between 1927 and 1947.)
Manager known for wearing 'spats' and overseeing the club for twenty years. During this time he managed three Wembley appearances including the FA Cup win in 1939. He retired in 1947 leaving a side ready to win the Championship in following years. Tinn died in March 1971 at the age of 93.

TODD, Ken

3 apps, 1 goal (1979-1980)
Career: *Wolves, Port Vale, Portsmouth (1976-1980).* Todd played four league games for Wolverhampton Wanderers before Port Vale broke their club record fee to buy him for £37,000 in August 1978. He failed to make a strong enough impression at Vale Park and and was sold on to Pompey for £20,000 in October 1979. Although he only played a few games for the club, he did return later and worked as youth team manager for four years. When he finally left the game, he set up a Tea Room in Chichester with his wife before moving back to his native north east. Now living in Bishop Auckland.

TODOROV, Svetoslav

83 apps, 33 goals (2002-2006)
Career: *Dobrudzha, Litex, West Ham United, Portsmouth, Wigan Athletic (loan), Charlton Athletic, Litex (1996-date).* Bulgarian international striker who enjoyed a purple patch at Pompey, scoring on average a goal for every two and a half games played and earing the Player of the Year award in 2002/3. He was signed by Harry Redknapp, for £750,000 in March 2002 - the manager obviously appreciated his ability having previously been his boss at West Ham. Having fallen out of the first team, he was given a free transfer and joined Charlton Athletic in July 2007. He is now back in Bulagaria playing for one of his former clubs, Litex Lovech
Player of the Year 2002-3

TOTTEN, Alex

4 apps (1994-1995)
Career: *Portsmouth, Bognor Regis Town (1994).* Made his Pompey debut in front of the TV cameras in 1994 but only played three more games before dropping into non-league football with Bognor Regis. Terry Fenwick had taken over as boss and immediately drafted in a clutch of experienced pros and Alex was one of the players chosen to make way for them. Returned to his home town, Southampton and gained his fork-lift truck license and a job at the container terminal.

TRAORE, Armand

28 apps, 1 goal (2008-2009)
Career: *Arsenal, Portsmouth (loan) (2006-date).* French youngster who impressed while on a season long loan in 2008. Now a regular member of Arsenal's first team squad and pushing for full international honours. He has already appeared for the French Under 19 and Under 21 sides.

TRAORE, Djimi

15 apps (2006-2008)
Career: *Laval, Liverpool, Lens (loan), Charlton Athletic, Portsmouth, Rennes (loan), Birmingham City (loan), AS Monaco (1996-date).* Former Liverpool defender, French-born Malian Traore was signed from Charlton by Harry Redknapp in a deal believed to be worth about £1million. On 18 June 2009 Traore signed a two-year deal with AS Monaco.

TRAVERS, Mike

88 apps, 6 goals (1967-1972)
Career: *Reading, Portsmouth, Aldershot, Basingstoke Town (1960-1972).*
Camberley born wing half who never ventured very far away from his birthplace. Initially, an apprentice with Reading, he signed for Pompey on a free transfer in January 1967. but his versatility meant that he was predominantly used as a substitute during his five year stay. Moved on to Aldershot at the end of the 1971/2 season and later player for Basingstoke Town before working as an accountant in Surrey until his retirement.

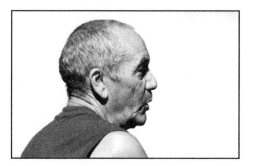

TREBILCOCK, Mike

123 apps, 37 goals (1967-1972)
Career: *Plymouth Argyle, Everton, Portsmouth, Torquay United, Weymouth (loan), Western Suburbs (1962-1976).*
'Trebilco' etched his name in the history books with two goals for Everton in the 1966 FA Cup Final and in doing so became the first black player to score in an FA Cup final. Originally from Cornwall, he played for Plymouth Argyle before moving to Goodison Park in a £23,000 transfer in December 1965. His stay on Merseyside lasted thee years but only saw him play 11 games for the first team. He moved to Pompey for a fee of £40,000 and scored a creditable 37 goals in his 123 appearances. The likable Cornishman returned to the south-west to play for Torquay and Weymouth before emigrating to Sydney, Australia. *Wrote an autobiography entitled "Dream, Believe, Achieve"*

TURNER, Andy

45 apps, 3 goals (1996-1998)
Career: *Tottenham Hotspur, Portsmouth, Crystal Palace, Rotherham United, Yeovil Town (1992-2002).* A former Tottenham youngster who has enjoyed a remarkable career and is still going strong, currently as player/manager of Chasetown in the Northern Premier League. He became the league's youngest scorer in 1992 when he found the net for Spurs against Everton. He joined Pompey for £250,000 four years later and his 45 appearances still rank as his highest total for one club even though he has played for over 20 league and non-league teams.

TURNER, Brian

4 apps (1969-1970)
Career: *Chelsea, Portsmouth, Brentford (1968-1971).* Only pulled on a Pompey jersey four times but he was a New Zealand international of repute who won over 100 international caps. Brian went on to play almost 100 games for Brentford but returned to New Zealand in 1972. He continued to play for a succession of clubs and was part of the country's 1982 World Cup squad. Turner also won three Player Of The Season Awards, was inducted into the National Hall of Fame and continued to coach once he finally retired from playing.

UNSWORTH, David

19 apps, 2 goals (2004-2005)
Career: *Everton, West Ham United, Aston Villa, Everton, Portsmouth, Ipswich Town (loan), Sheffield United, Wigan Athletic, Burnley, Huddersfield Town (1991-2009).*
Despite a career that spanned over 400 league appearances, most at the top level and an England call up, Unsworth is probably as well remembered for a fateful move to Aston Villa in 1998. Having joined the club from West Ham for £3 million in the close season, he left without making an appearance and re-joined his first club, Everton. The tabloid press had a field day, accusing him of being 'under the thumb'. In the light of this it is somewhat surprising that he agreed to move much further south to join Pompey in 2004. His stay was relatively brief and despite scoring a couple of important penalties, he returned north to sign for Sheffield United. In 2008, Unsworth was appointed player-coach at Huddersfield Town, however he left this position and subsequently retired the following year. He was appointed development coach at Preston North End shortly afterwards, but soon after was promoted to first team coach.

UPRICHARD, Norman

195 apps (1952-1959)
Career: *Arsenal, Swindon Town, Portsmouth, Southend United (1948-1959).* Eddie Lever's first signing as Pompey manager, Norman Uprichard had already been capped by Northern Ireland when he put pen to paper in 1952. Arsenal had brought 'Black Jake' over to England in 1948 but an he failed to break into their first team. and was allowed to join Swindon for £750 in 1949. It was there that he blossomed into an international keeper and attracted the interest of bigger clubs (Pompey!). Described as 'diminutive but fearless', he played nearly 200 first-team games for the Blues in seven seasons and was a fans' favourite. Many will remember throwing sweets into his goal, which he would duly enjoy during the game. Norman ended his playing days at Southend United and became licensee of the Belmont Hotel in Hastings before moving back to Belfast to run the Queens University bar. However, when he finally retired it was the lure of the Sussex coast that encouraged him to settle back in Hastings to enjoy an active retirement.

VAUGHAN, Charlie

28 apps, 16 goals (1952-1954)
Career: *Charlton Athletic, Portsmouth (1945-1953).* A veteran centre forward signed from Charlton in 1953 - played 28 games and scored an impressive 16 goals - including a hat-trick in a 5-2 Fratton win over Huddersfield. Charlie was an England B international but sadly died in March 1989.

Photo: Sicknote10

VERNAZZA, Paolo

7 apps (1999-2000)
Career: *Arsenal, Ipswich T, Portsmouth (loan), Watford, Rotherham U,(1997-date).* An England under 21 international, Vernazza made seven consecutive appearances for Pompey during a loan spell in 1999/2000. He was registered as an Arsenal player at the time and did appear at the highest level for the Gunners. Now playing in non-league football and he joined his current club Hemel Hempstead Town in March 2010.

VIAFARA, Jhon

15 apps, 1 goal (2005-2006)
Career: *Portsmouth, Real Sociedad (loan), Southampton, Once Caldas, Juan Aurich (1999-date).* A tall and athletic Colombian midfielder Viáfara made his name with Once Caldas, for whom he was instrumental during his club's success in the Copa Libertadores, the South American version of the UEFA Champions League. This earned him a £800,000 move to Pompey at the beginning of the 2005-06 season. After playing in several games during the first half of the season, he was dropped by Harry Redknapp who had returned from his brief break up the M27 and loaned out to Spanish Primera División club Real Sociedad. In the August he signed a three year deal with Southampton. for a fee believed to be in the region of £750,000. Two seasons later he was on the plane back home to re-sign for his first club. but signed for Bogota based Club Deportivo La Equidad Seguros in 2010.

VIGNAL, Gregory

17 apps (2005-2006)
Career: *Montpellier, Liverpool, Portsmouth, , Southampton, Birmingham City (1999-date).* French Under 21 international whose UK career was triggered by a £500,000 move to Liverpool from Montpellier. He lasted five seasons with the Reds but only played 11 first team games before being released on a free transfer. He had been loaned out to a number of clubs including Rangers but decided to join Pompey instead of the Scottish giants. This decision may have been regretted when Harry Redknapp returned to the club and was clearly not a Vignal fan. After tree years back in France, he played one season for Birmingham and since September 2010 has been on the books of Greek side Atromitos.

Photo: EchetusXe

VINCENT, Jamie

49 apps, 1 goal (2000-2002)
Career: *Crystal Palace, Bournemouth, Huddersfield Town, Portsmouth, Walsall (loan), Derby County, Millwall, Yeovil Town, Swindon Town, Walsall (1993-date).* Jamie first made a real impression in league football while on loan to Bournemouth from Crystal Palace in the mid 1990's.

He has since played for ten clubs including a three year stint at Pompey between 2001 and 2004. an £800,000 capture from Huddersfield Town, he made 49 appearances and scored one goal before moving on to Derby County. Most recently, he signed a deal with Aldershot Town in September 2010 following his release from Swindon Town , both clubs being within easy travelling distance from his Berkshire home.

VINE, Rowan

13 apps (2000-2002)
Career: *Portsmouth, Brentford (loan), Colchester United (loan), Luton Town, Birmingham City, Queens Park Rangers (2000-date).* Vine was a product of the Pompey youth set-up but struggled to force his way into the first team. Joined Luton Town in July 2005 for about £250,000 and became an instant hit. Consistent performances and a hatful of goals earned a £3.5 million move to Birmingham less than 18 months later. The midland side had just earned promotion to the Premiership but this proved to be a step too far for the Basingstoke born striker. He was loaned to Queens Park Rangers and eventually joined them permanently. In October 2010 the London club agreed to lend him to Hull City and ironically, one of his first games was against Pompey.

Guilty or innocent?

VINEY, Keith

194 apps, 3 goals (1976-1982)

Career: *Portsmouth, Exeter City, Torquay United (loan), Bristol Rovers (loan) (1975-1988).* Spotted by Ray Crawford while still at the Technical High School, Viney, who had always been a Pompey fan, realised his dream made his first team debut in 1976. He had joined the club at a time when Ian St John was forced to rely on a clutch of youngsters and was given his chance alongside Steve Foster and Chris Kamara. The next six years were full of ups and downs: he had to endure relegation to the fourth division, was called upon to play in goal during two matches, and was Player of the Year in 1980/1. After almost 200 games in all competitions, he joined Exeter City, where became a fans' favourite and was voted their Player of The Year twice. Upon retirement, he helped Torrington, firstly as manager, then as Director of Football. Still living in Devon and working in the financial services industry training new financial advisers. *Alan Knight is married to his sister!*

Photo: Mikhail Slain

VLACHOS, Michalis

64 apps, 1 goal (1997-2000)

Career: *Apollon Smyrnis, Olympiakos, AEK Athens, Portsmouth, Walsall, Ionikos, Apollon Smyrnis (1985-2003).* Already a full international, Vlachos became Alan Ball's first signing and the first Greek to play for the club when he joined on a 'Bosman' free transfer in 1998. He immediately added grit to the midfield and managed to help avoid impending relegation from the First Division. Joined Walsall two years later before returning home to start a career in management with amateur side Apollon Eretrias. Since 2008, he has been in charge at Peramaikos.

VUKIC, Zvonimir

9 apps, 1 goal (2005-2006)

Career: *Shakhtar Donetsk, Portsmouth (loan), Partizan (loan), FC Moscow (1994-date).* Serbian international midfielder who played nine games on loan from Shakhtar Doneetsk in 2005/6. When Alain Perrin was sacked, Vukic soon found himself on a plane home. He played on loan for FK Partizan and then signed for current club, FC Moscow, in 2008.

WALDON, Keith

(Caretaker manager January 1998.)

Former Assistant Manager to Terry Fenwick and was briefly caretaker manager. His tenure was brief and consisted of three defeats, before Alan Ball was appointed as Manager in January 1998. He is a sports coach and became Vice Chairman of The Society of Sports Therapists.

WALDRON, Malcolm

24 apps, 1 goal (1983-1985)

Career: *Southampton, Burnley, Portsmouth (1974-1986).* Emsworth born Waldron was a former England under 23 international who spent nine years with Southampton. He missed out on their 1976 FA Cup win but won an England 'B' cap following a string of impressive performances. He ended up at Fratton Park in 1983 after failing to settle 'up north' with Burnley. His calming influence helped to shore up a leaky defence but injury brought his career to a premature end in 1985. He became an advertising sales representative in Portsmouth and sold double glazing before moving onto Abbey Life and is now a Health Care advisor for BUPA in Poole.

WALKER, Harry

57 apps (1938-1947)
Career: *Darlington, Portsmouth, Nottingham Forest (1935-1954).* "Harry" Walker was the goalkeeper in the team that beat Wolves 4–1 in the 1939 FA Cup Final. He was a trained motor mechanic which meant that he could remain in the area to work in the Naval Dockyard during the Second World War - and could also mind Pompey's goal throughout the 'war' years. Nicknamed the 'Cat' long before anyone had heard of Peter Bonetti, Harry went on to play almost 300 games for Notts Forest before retiring. He died in 1976.

WALSH, Paul

113 apps, 26 goals (1992-1996)
Career: *Charlton Athletic, Luton Town, Liverpool, Tottenham Hotspur, Queens Park Rangers, Portsmouth, Manchester City, Portsmouth (1979-1996).* An England international striker who was one of the top strikers of his day and it could be argued that the highlights of his career include his England caps and starring roles with several top clubs. However, during his time at Fratton Park, he became a true hero and earned a place in Pompey fans' hearts forever. Jim Smith paid Spurs a mere £400,000 to plug the gap left by Darren Anderton's £1.7m move to the same London club. In the first of two spells, his mesmerising displays frequently resulted in goalscoring opportunities for Guy Whittingham.

Despite Whittingham's record haul of goals in 1992/3, promotion was missed by the smallest of margins and Walshie's only consolation was being voted Player of the Year. The following year Jim Smith sold him to Manchester City for £750,000. Much to the delight of the local population, he was wearing a blue shirt again 18 months later when Terry Fenwick brought him back to the club. This second spell was to only last five months as he suffered a knee injury in a game against Leicester City and was forced to retire. He became a players' agent, TV pundit and an ambassador for FIFA. Walshie also appears regularly for the Liverpool veterans side, often forming a deadly partnership with fellow Pompey old boy John Durnin.
Player of the season in 1993.

WAPENAAR, Harald

8 apps (2003-2004)
Career: *Feyenoord, RBC Roosendaal, Helmond Sport, FC Utrecht, Udinese, Portsmouth, Vitesse, Sparta Rotterdam (1988-2009).* Dutch goalkeeper arrived from FC Utrecht in the summer of 2003 as understudy to Shaka Hislop. Has been with Sparta Rotterdam since returning to his homeland at the end of the 200/7 season.

PLAY UP POMPEY!

WATERMAN, David

88 apps (1996-2001)
Career: *Portsmouth, Oxford United (1995-2004).* A Northern Ireland international although he was born in Guernsey and a lifetime Pompey fan. Initially signed as a YTS apprentice he captained the youth team and and won Young Player of the Year. Signed pro terms in 1995 and went on play under six different managers. Sadly, a series of niggling injuries combined with changing managerial preferences, his first team chances were limited and ultimately resulted in a move to Oxford United in 2001. Now lives in Gosport and has started the Oakley Waterman Caravan Foundation, which provides an escape for parents whose children have been diagnosed with cancer. The charity is named after his own son Oakley who died from rhabdomysarcoma, a rare form of cancer, at the age of six.
Dave's uncle's house is called 'Fratton End'

WEBB, Neil

139 apps, 38 goals (1982-1985)
Career: *Reading, Portsmouth, Nottingham Forest, Manchester United, Nottingham Forest, Swindon Town, Grimsby Town, Aldershot (1980-1997).* Followed his father's footsteps and started at home town club Reading. Bobby Campbell paid £83,000 and had to fight off stiff competition to bring the youngster to Fratton Park in June 1982. This was a large sum for the club at the time, particularly as Webb was still a teenager and relatively unproven. Three years later he had blossomed into a future international and it was no surprise when he was lured away to a 'bigger' club. Brian Cough parted with £250,000 and a move to Nottingham Forest was sealed. Webb went on to play for Manchester United and win 26 England caps before his career came to an end at Aldershot. A brief managerial career with Weymouth and Reading Town followed but this proved to be short lived. Sadly, he fell upon hard times and has since worked as a postman and for a transport company in Reading. His ex-wife Shelley Webb became a TV presenter, becoming a real footballers' wives interviewee, and then wrote the book called Footballers' Wives. Their two sons are both playing football, Luke joined Hereford United while Josh stayed closer to home with Basingstoke Town.
Player of the season in 1985.

WEDDLE, Derek

24apps, 8 goals (1956-1959)
Career: *Sunderland, Portsmouth, Middlesbough, Darlington, York (1955-1966).* Spotted by a Sunderland scout and signed for the Wearside club in 1953. Imposing goal scorer who scored 8 goals in his 24 matches in Blue. Later dropped down to non-league soccer and once scored seven goals in a match for Cambridge City. Later ran a dairy business and then took over a newsagents'. Helped in a school's sports department but retired in 2000.

Johnnie Phillips and Ray Crawford

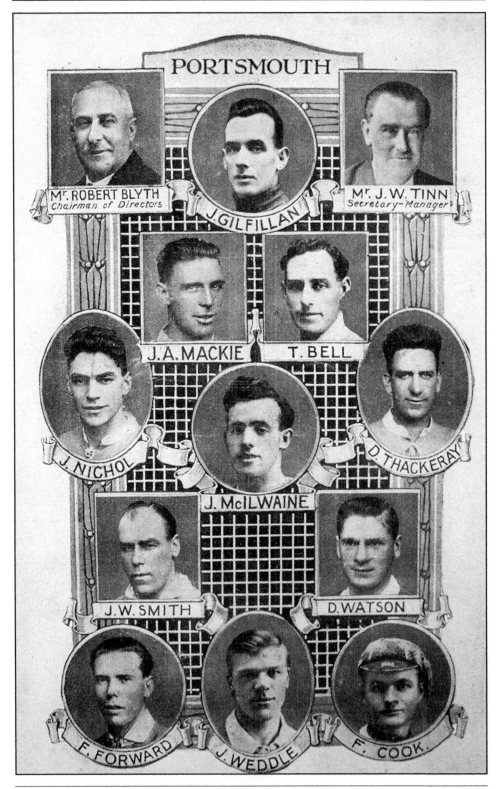

PORTSMOUTH

Mr. ROBERT BLYTH
Chairman of Directors

J. GILFILLAN

Mr. J. W. TINN
Secretary-Manager

J. A. MACKIE

T. BELL

J. NICHOL

J. McILWAINE

D. THACKERAY

J. W. SMITH

D. WATSON

F. FORWARD

J. WEDDLE

F. COOK.

WEDDLE, Jack 'Dixie'

368 apps, 171 goals (1927-1937)
Career: *Portsmouth, Blackburn Rovers (1927-1939).* Pompey's leading scorer for six seasons who bagged 171 goals in his eleven years at Fratton Park. A former miner, 'Dixie' later became a trainer at Blackburn and died in November 1979.

WENT, Paul

109 apps, 6 goals (1973-1976)
Career: *Leyton Orient, Charlton Athletic, Fulham, Portsmouth, Cardiff City, Orient (1966-1980).* London born Went was hailed as a star in the making and had played for both the England Schoolboys and Youth side before the age of 17. When John Deacon took over as Chairman at Fratton Park, Went was seen as a rock upon which to build a side that could challenge for honours and the club. A fee of £155,000 was agreed with Charlton Athletic, a massive sum for a small club in those days and Went signed in December 1973. The money seemed to be well spent as he performed heroically and was named fans' Player of the Year in 1974. The side failed to live up to the Chairman's high expectations and bit by bit was sold off to recoup some of the money invested. Went was sold to Cardiff City in October 1976 for only £30,000. After only a year in Wales, Went returned to the capital and eventually moved into coaching with his first club, Orient. He now lives near Chelmsford in Essex and has worked as a publican and a sales rep for a brewery. *Player of the season in 1974.*

Photo: Bart Hurkens

WESTERVELD, Sander

7 apps (2005-2006)
Career: *Liverpool, Real Sociedad, Mallorca (loan), Portsmouth, Everton (loan), Almería, Sparta Rotterdam, Monza (1994-date).* Liverpool broke the transfer record for a goalkeeper when they parted with £4 million to bring Westerveld into English football in 2000. Ironically, he was bought to replace David James. Having played a major part in the Reds' Treble winning season his form dipped and new manager Gérard Houllier allowed him to leave. Spells with Real Sociedad and Mallorca followed before Alain Perrin persuaded him to return to the UK in July 2005. Was initially first choice for but struggled to find consistency. After a loan period at Everton was released in May 2006. He then helped Spanish second Division side UD Almería gain promotion before returning to Holland. Joined Italian side A.C. Monza Brianza 1912, in the summer of 2009.

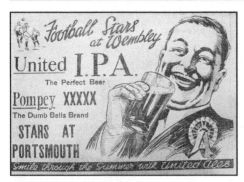

WHARTON, Guy

73 apps, 5 goals (1938-1948)
Career: *Chester, Wolverhampton Wanderers, Portsmouth, Darlington (1935-1949).*
Acquired from Wolves in November 1937, Guy played left half for the Pompey team that defeated his former club in the 1939 FA Cup final. Like so many of his peers, the Second World War took away what may been some of his best playing years. Although he did regain his position in the side in 1946 he was replaced fairly quickly by Jimmy Scoular and was allowed to join Darlington in 1948. Had a spell as a trainer at Watford before taking on a career away from football with the Goodyear Tyre Company. He died in 1990.

WHITE, Jim

31 apps 6 goals (1958-1961)
Career: *Bournemouth, Portsmouth, Gillingham, Bournemouth, Cambridge United (1957-1971)* Jim is a Dorset born centre forward who followed manager Freddie Cox from club to club. He made his debut at Bournemouth and Cox brought him to Pompey the following year. He went on to play over 300 games for four league clubs, three of which were under his first boss. Later became player-coach at Cambridge United and had a spell in Finland. White worked as a Theatre Assistant at Addenbrookes hospital in Cambridge until his retirement.

WHITEBREAD, Adrian

158 apps, 3 goals (1995-2000)
Career: *Leyton Orient, Swindon Town, West Ham United, Portsmouth, Luton Town (loan), Reading, Exeter City (loan). (1989-2003).*
Whitbread joined Pompey for £250,000 in October 1996 following a successful loan spell. Became captain and mainstay of the defence until he had to undergo knee surgery in the summer of 2000. He was never able to regain his first-team slot. Is currently the Assistant Coach of the Puerto Rico National Team and the Puerto Rico Islanders.

Paul Walsh and Guy Whittingham with Pompey author and toastmaster Roger Holmes

WHITEHEAD, Clive

74 apps, 2 goals (1987-1989)
Career: *Bristol City, West Bromwich Albion, Wolverhampton Wanderers, Portsmouth, Exeter City (1973-1990).* Birmingham born midfielder who had made almost 400 league appearances for Bristol City and West Brom before bringing his experience to the Pompey team in 1987. He joined on a free transfer and during his two years at the club proved to be a valuable asset, being able to play in a number of positions before leaving for Exeter City in 1989. Became manager of Yeovil Town, returned to Bristol City as Reserve/Youth coach and then joined the PFA as a financial advisor. Clive now works as a fully qualified Financial Adviser with Openwork.
Helped Bristol City win promotion to the first division in 1976 scoring the promotion winning goal against Pompey!

WHITTINGHAM, Guy

225 apps, 115 goals (1989-1993 & 1998-2001)
Career: *Yeovil Town, Portsmouth, Aston Villa, Wolverhampton Wanderers (loan), Sheffield Wednesday, Wolverhampton Wanderers (loan), Portsmouth (loan), Watford (loan), Portsmouth, Peterborough United (loan), Oxford United (loan), Wycombe Wanderers (1988-2001).* 'Corporal Punishment' made over 450 appearances for a number of clubs, after leaving the British Army at the ripe old age of 25. Despite this relatively late start, he notched up over 100 Pompey goals and broke the club's all-time scoring record of 42 league goals in the 1992-3 season. He also featured in the FA Cup semi final against Liverpool in 1992. History was to repeat itself, when as a Wycombe Wanderers player he suffered the fate and at the hands of the same opponents. He later went on to become player-manager of Newport, Isle of Wight, but left them in 2005 when the club ran into financial difficulties. He also coached at Newbury and Eastleigh before joining the first-team coaching staff at Fratton Park in January 2009.
Player of the season in 1990.

WIDDOWSON, Bob

4 apps (1969-1970)
Career: *Sheffield United, York City, Portsmouth (1961-1969).* The first player that Pompey ever signed on loan, Widdowson was York City's reserve keeper when called in to cover for the injured John Milkins. Later coached the juniors at Sheffield United's academy.

WIGLEY, Steve

140 apps, 12 goals (1988-1993)
Career: *Nottingham Forest, Sheffield United, Birmingham City, Portsmouth, Exeter City (1982-1993).* The former Notts Forest winger was a transfer deadline day signing in 1989. Having had first division experience, John Gregory saw him as the man to provide ammunition to the forward line and parted with £300,000 to bring him in from Birmingham City. Gave four years loyal service before Jim Smith allowed him to join Exeter City on a free transfer. He then dropped down to non-league football to gain coaching and management experience at Aldershot, with whom he won the Guardian Insurance League Cup in 1995/6. Has since held positions with a number of clubs and was at one time part of the England Under 21 set up. Joined Bristol City as assistant manager in August 2010.

WILLIAMS, Bill

3 apps (1960-1961)
Career: *Portsmouth, Queens Park Rangers, West Bromwich Albion, Mansfield Town, Gillingham (1960-1971).* Bill only made three appearances in a Pompey shirt, having joined the club as a fifteen year old. He but went on to play for four other league clubs. He later had a long association with Maidstone United, which included three separate spells as manager. He is currently the club's general manager and a shareholder. Williams previously managed Dover Athletic in the Football Conference as well as Kingstonian.

WILLIAMSON, Mike

0 apps (2008-2009)
Career: *Torquay United, Southampton, Wycombe Wanderers, Watford, Portsmouth, Newcastle United (2001-date)*. Williamson was at the centre of a bizarre tale that illustrated the financial turmoil that he club were in. Paul Hart desperately needed re-enforcements and persuaded Watford to sell their 'star' defender, (who had previously been released by Southampton on a free transfer having been unable to break into their first team) for an initial fee in the region of £2 million. However, he was sold on to Newcastle United in January 2010, without having made one appearance, for fear that it would trigger a clause that meant that a further £1 million would have to be paid. He has since established himself in the heart of the Newcastle defence and was awarded the 'man of the match' award on his debut.

WILSON, Alex

382 apps, 5 goals (1951-1967)
Career: *Portsmouth (1949-1967)*. Scottish defender who joined Pompey on leaving school in 1949, turning professional the following year, and played for 18 years, winning a Division 3 championship in 1962. In 1967 he moved to Chelmsford City for a short spell before retiring. He won one cap for Scotland and played almost 400 club games retiring. Alex continued to live in the area and worked as a print representative. He eventually returned to Inverness in Scotland and died there on 29th July 2010.

WILSON, Billy

216 apps, 6 goals (1971-1979)
Career: *Blackburn Rovers, Portsmouth (1964-1978)*. Originally from the North East, Billy and his wife agreed to move south from Blackburn Rovers in 1972 with a plan to only stay for two years. Not only did the the fair haired defender/midfielder play over 200 times for the club over eight years, he still lives in the area, almost forty years later. Despite training to run a garage in preparation for his retirement, he went straight into into the pub trade, initially becoming licensee of the Pompey, which used to be on Frogmore Road, just outside Fratton Park. Thirteen years at the Three Tuns

in Gosport followed and he has now returned to the town to enjoy his retirement after stints at the Wyvern at Lee-on-the-Solent and the Horse and Jockey in Curbridge.

WILSON, Scott

5 apps (2001-2002)
Career: *Rangers, Portsmouth (loan), Dunfermline Athletic, North Queensland Fury (1993-date)*. Joined Pompey on loan in 2001/2 in the hope of winning a permanent contract but returned to his parent club Rangers after only five appearances. A Scottish under 21 international, Wilson joined Australian team North Queensland Fury in March 2009.

WIMBLETON, Paul

10 apps (1981-1984)
Career: *Portsmouth, Cardiff City, Bristol City, Shrewsbury Town, Exeter City, Swansea City. (1981-1993)*. Havant born midfielder who managed to notch up over 200 league appearances despite fighting injuries for most of his career. Later won the Welsh Cup twice as a Barry Town player, played in South Africa, Hong Kong, in Ireland for Cork City, China and finally back to Wales with Merthyr Tydfil. Paul then moved to the States initially as player for the Delaware Wizards and Hampton Roads Mariners in the 'A' League in the United States . In 1998 Wimbleton started his own soccer coaching business, Three Lions Soccer Academy, in New Jersey.

WOLLEASTON, Rob

6 apps (2000-2001)
Career: *Chelsea, Bristol Rovers (loan), Nottingham Forest (loan), Portsmouth (loan), Northampton Town (loan), Bradford City, Oxford United, Cambridge United, Rushden & Diamonds (1998-date)*. Former Chelsea youngster who made first team appearances for the Stamford Road club and had short loan spells with Bristol Rovers, Nottingham Forest, Northampton Town and Pompey. Following his release from Chelsea, he played for Bradford City and Oxford United before dropping into non-league football with Cambridge United. Moved to Rushden & Diamonds in 2008 but is currently looking for a new club.

When Portsmouth won the Cup in 1939, Worrall, their outside-right, played throughout the final with a small horse-shoe in his pocket, a sprig of heather in each stocking, and a white elephant charm tied to one garter.

WOOD, Paul

90 apps, 11 goals (1982-1987 and 1993-1996)
Career: *Portsmouth, Brighton, Sheffield U, Bournemouth, Portsmouth (1982-2003).* A right-sided attacking midfielder who had two spells at Fratton Park. Initially signed pro terms in 1981 and returned twelve years later having played for Brighton, Sheffield United and Bournemouth in the intervening years. After two seasons as a versatile squad player, Paul moved over to Hong Kong, where he was the First Division league's leading scorer in the 1997–98 season. On his return he joined Havant & Waterlooville and was their Player of the Year in 2002. Now lives in Bournemouth where he worked as a painter & decorator before studying to be a financial adviser.

WORRALL, Fred

47 apps (1938-1939)
Career: *Oldham Athletic, Portsmouth, Crewe Alexandra, Stockport County (1928-1945).* Fred Worrall was capped twice for England and was the only player from the 1934 FA Cup final side to play for the Pompey team that beat Wolves 4–1 in the 1939 FA Cup Final. He later became a trainer at Chester and Warrington Rugby League club and managed Stockton Heath in Cheshire. Fred died in April 1979 at the age of 68

YEBDA, Hassan

18 apps 2 goals (2009-2010)
The Algerian international midfielder is now playing in Italy for S.S.C. Napoli.

YEO, Brian

2 apps (1962-1963)
Career: *Portsmouth, Gillingham (1961-1975).* Brian spent almost his entire career playing for Gillingham, for whom he holds the all-time record for the most goals scored in the Football League. He had graduated through the junior ranks at Portsmouth but never made a first-team appearance before Freddie Cox signed him for the Gills in 1963. In 1975 Yeo retired from professional football to concentrate on running a newsagent's in the town, but also had spells managing Folkestone and Canterbury City. In 2004, after ten years as a driver for the local paper, Brian retired to spend more time on the golf course.

YEULL, Jasper

35 apps (1947-1949)
Career: *Portsmouth, Barnsley (1946-1952).* After emerging from the junior ranks of West Brom, Yeuell signed professional forms with Pompey in 1946. He was a member of the championship winning team of 1949 and 1950. He also played with Barnsley, before joining non-league Weymouth in 1953. When his career was ended by injury, Yeuell settled in Hastings, Sussex where he worked as a self-employed decorator. He passed away in July 2003.

YOULDEN, Tommy

95 apps, 1 goal (1968-1972)
Career: *Arsenal, Portsmouth, Reading, Aldershot (1965-1980).* Youlden began his career as an apprentice at Arsenal but did not make a first team game before moving to Pompey in April 1968. In a little over three seasons made 95 appearances. Signed for Reading in time for the 72/3 season, and then played for Aldershot for four years. Left the 'Shots' at the end of 80/1 and ended his career at Addlestone & Weybridge. Returned to live in his native North London. Taught economics, politics as well as football at University College School in Hampstead.Also helped out at Chelsea's academy for three years.

ZIVKOVIC, Boris

20 apps (2003-2004)
Career: *Bayer Leverkusen, Portsmouth, VfB Stuttgart, 1 Fc Koln (loan), Hajduk Split (1994-2009).* Croatian defender who spent six seasons with Bayer Leverkusen before joining Pompey in the summer of 2003. He was a first team regular until he fell out with Harry Redknapp and was allowed to return to Germany, this time with VfB Stuttgart. He also managed to upset Niko Kranjcar's dad who was the Croatian national team manager for the 2002 World cup. Zivkovic gave away a penalty against Mexico, was sent off and Mexico scored from the spot to secure a 1-0 win. In August 2006 he moved to Hajduk Split.

ZAJEC, Velimir

(Manager between Nov 2004 and April 2005). Zalec was a Yugoslav international midfielder who represented his country 40 times as a player. He had moved into management with Panathanaikos and Dynamo Zagreb before accepting an offer to become Pompey's Director of Football in 2004. His lively stay included a brief spell as temporary team manager after Harry Redknapp's resignation. The position was made permanent in December 2004, but after only five months he reverted back to his director's role. He resigned from this position in the following October. After five years out of the limelight he recently re-emerged when appointed manager of Dynamo Zagreb in May 2010.

ZAMPERINI, Alessandro

17 apps, 2 goals (2001-2002)
Career: *Portsmouth, Modena, Acireale, Sambenedettese, Ternana, Cisco Roma, Valle del Giovenco, FK Ventspils, Ravenna Calcio (2001-date).* Italian defender who played 17 games in the 2001-2 season having joined from Roma, the club he had supported as a child. Apart from a short stint in Latvia with FK Ventspils, he has spent the years since in the lower reaches of the Italian league and is currently playing for Ravenna Calcio in Italy's Lega Pro Prima Divisione (third division).

Pompey websites

To keep up to date with everything to do with Pompey, including present and former players, why not visit these websites...

Portsmouth FC Official Site
www.portsmouthfc.co.uk
Portsmouth News
www.portsmouth.co.uk
Pompey Chimes
www.pompeychimes.net
Pompeyrama
http://pompeyrama.com
Fratton Faithful
www.portsmouth-mad.co.uk
Vital Pompey
www.portsmouth.vitalfootball.co.uk
Pompey Online
www.pompeyonline.com
The Pompey Trust
www.pompeytrust.com
Pompey Til I Die
www.pompeytillidie.com

...and don't miss Bygone Blues in the Football Mail every Saturday.

Also available now

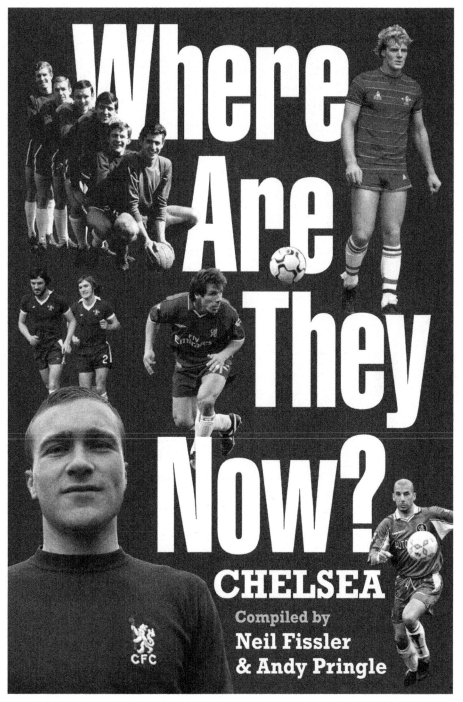

Where Are They Now - Chelsea (ISBN 9780955493751)
See a sample chapter at www.where-are-they-now.co.uk/chelsea

Also available now

Where Are They Now - United (ISBN 9780955493744)
See a sample chapter at www.where-are-they-now.co.uk/manchester-united

Visit our website

www.where-are-they-now.co.uk

If you enjoyed this book, we hope that you will also like our website.
If you know what happened to any players, we would love to hear from you.

Acknowledgments

Many thanks to Jake Payne, Pat Neil, Leigh Edwards, Roger Holmes, Neil Fissler, Andi Saunders, Nigel Standerline, Phil (Pompeyrama), Ann Boere, and all the former players who have been kind enough to help.

Bibliography

Pompey Players 1920-2001
Roger Holmes
Pompey People
Mick Cooper
(Yore Publications)
Curse of the Jungle Boy
Ray Crawford with Michael Wood
(PB Publishing)
Pompey - The History
Neasom, Cooper & Robinson
(Milestone Publications)
The PFA Premier League and Football League Record 1949-1998
Hugman, Barry J.
(Lennard Queen Anne Press)
An English Football Internationals Who's who
Lamming, D. (Hutton Press)
Breedon Book of Football Managers
Turner, Dennis and White Alex.
(Breedon Sports Books)
Where Are They Now?
Pringle Andy, Fissler, Neil.
(Two Heads Publishing)

Photographs

A really big thank you to Jake Payne, whose photographic collection has helped bring this book to life. Many of the images have come from former players' own collections and I am extremely grateful for their co-operation.

Cover photos

David Streten Photography, Cosham
Associated Sports Photography
Mirrorpix, London, Jake Payne

Other photographs

Adam Hutt
www.flickr.com/photos/adam_hutt
Bart Hurkens
www.flickr.com/photos/28240695@N06
Ben Angel
www.flickr.com/photos/benangel
Ben Sutherland
www.flickr.com/photos/bensutherland
buster1976
www.flickr.com/photos/buster1976
Camw
commons.wikimedia.org/wiki/User:Camw
choonming
www.flickr.com/photos/choonming
cultzeros
www.flickr.com/photos/cultzeros
dalli58
www.flickr.com/photos/dalli
Dan Mullen
www.flickr.com/photos/dan_mullen
EchetusXe
en.wikipedia.org/wiki/User:EchetusXe
Egghead06
en.wikipedia.org/wiki/User:Egghead06
Mikhail Slain
foto.mail.ru/mail/michael_62
Paxie
www.flickr.com/photos/paxie
Rockface
www.flickr.com/photos/rockface
Sir Pix-A -Lot
www.flickr.com/photos/a_ndrew
stubramley
www.flickr.com/photos/stubramley/3706247749
The Reeds and torkst
http://liverpool.no
Thiago Piccoli
www.flickr.com/photos/tomatemaravilha
Tobreatheasone
www.flickr.com/photos/tobreatheasone
TuborgLight
commons.wikimedia.org/wiki/User:TuborgLight
TwntiethApril1986
en.wikipedia.org/wiki/User:TwentiethApril1986
wjarrettc
www.flickr.com/photos/wjarrettc

...and to anyone else who knows me!